Gentlemen in Blue

The Story of George Ransley and the Aldington Gang (the Blues)

By
Lyn Watts

Lyn Watts
x

Gentlemen in Blue

First Published January 2018
First Reprint April 2018

10 9 8 7 6 5 4 3 2 1

Copyright © Lyn Watts 2018

ISBN 978-0-9932977-2-4

Printed by Print Domain, 107 High Street, Thurnscoe, Rotherham, S. Yorks S63 0QZ

Published by: WattKnott Publishing, Testers, Whatlington, Battle TN33 0NS England

Gentlemen in Blue

CONTENTS

In the Beginning	v
The Bourne Tap	2
The Roaring Ransleys	14
The Blues	26
Cousins	32
Murder on Dover beach	38
Taken in the night	44
Custody and court	51
All are gathered in	56
A final farewell	61
Trial at Maidstone	67
Life without love	76
Transportation	80
After the Blues	90
What happened next	94
The last word	116
Bibliography	122
About the author	123

In the Beginning

I first became interested in the South Kent smugglers (or Aldington Gang as they became known) when I was asked to write short stories for a fortnightly publication on the Romney Marshes in Kent. My earliest scribbles were pure fiction and forged from my overdeveloped imagination. However, I soon became interested in the area itself with its mediaeval churches. Looking for inspiration one day, I spotted the galleon painted onto the wall of St Dunstan's Church, Snargate. I learned that this was believed to be a sign to smugglers that the church was a safe storage place for uncustomed goods. I began reading about smuggling in the area and, from there, became hooked on the Aldington gang, with a particular interest in its leader, George Ransley. My first book - 'Traders of the Fifth Continent – Tales of

Smugglers and Rascals on the Romney Marshes' - contained short stories. These were mainly about smugglers, largely the Aldington Gang. The Rascally brothers of Ruckinge were also featured. These were George Ransley's elder cousins. There was also a purely fictional story in that publication.

This time I wanted to write something more factual, but in a form that was not too dry and 'text book'; something which would appeal to all tastes and levels of interest in the subject. In order to capture the character of George Ransley, and to re-create the atmosphere of those times, I invented one fictional person. All the others were real and lived, at that time, in or around the Aldington area. Essentially all of the facts are true.

I have used a little poetic license in mounting George on horseback. He may have been able to ride but it is unlikely he would have ridden much. Contemporary reports from the time report him as going everywhere driving his horse and cart. Most carters and ploughman would ride sideways on the horses back coming in from the fields and that would usually be all the riding they would do.

Lord Teignmouth, in his book 'The Smugglers', had many an interview with an unidentified nonagenarian who, finding himself financially distressed, finished his days in Aldington workhouse. As a boy, had been a tub carrier for the gang. Much of the information on them comes from him. My own researches believe him to be a certain

James Slingsby, born on the 20th of May 1804. He lived all his life in Aldington and died on the 3rd of January 1895. He is buried in Aldington churchyard.

I enjoyed immensely my research for this book and doubtless would have found it far harder work, maybe even impossible, without the use of the internet. This made me appreciate even more, the works of people such as John Douch and Henry Shore, Lord Teignmouth. They had to rely on travel, correspondence and slogging through parish (or Admiralty) records for their information.

The fascination in finding the journals of the ship's surgeon on line, or seeing the hand written reports from the Tasmanian records office on the convicts and their physical descriptions, gave me as much pleasure as the writing of the book itself. I found it amazing that I was able to discover the colour of their hair, their eyes and how tall they were almost two hundred years later. Indeed, I felt bereft once I had finished the book, as I no longer had an excuse to peruse those pages.

In their day, the gang would not have been known by the name "Blues". That epithet was given to them later. The reason is lost in the mists of time but it was possibly for the dark blue gabardines, or smocks, that they wore so as to blend better into the night, or possibly for the blue flares they used to warn the boats bringing the contraband not to land if the Blockade force were about. For my purposes in this story, I shall refer to them as the Blues.

Aldington, and the surrounding area, has changed somewhat since George Ransley's day but his home, The Bourne Tap, still stands, although it has been extended and is now a respectable private house. The Walnut Tree Inn is still a popular, busy hostelry serving very good food and drink. Cephas Quested's cottage is still standing in the Frith road, Aldington. I suspect it is somewhat larger these days than in Cephas' time. Most moving of all is the Ransley grave board in Ruckinge churchyard, marking the burial site of the Rascally Brothers and other family members.

The area may have changed but I think, were he to return, George would still recognise it and feel at home in it. One cannot visit the area without feeling the history in the very atmosphere. I feel closer to those characters when I am in the Romney, or Walland, Marsh area or in the villages of Aldington, Bilsington, Bonnington, Mersham and Ruckinge.

I think, whatever your view of the crimes of the Blues, it has to be taken in the context of the hard, and often violent, times in which they lived. There would not have been the need for violence if the government had not made a crime out of that which never should have been! Some of the punishments meted out by the legal system of the day were far harsher than anything returned by George and his batsmen. Life was a constant struggle for the rural working man. Death by hanging was the usual punishment awaiting any man who was caught running smuggled goods. Working men needed to improve their lot, and that of their families, but, naturally, they had an incentive to protect themselves from capture.

One of the highlights of my research came when looking for *The Hatch at Mersham. I wanted to see the house and grounds, albeit from a distance, when, to my delight, my long suffering husband and I found that the Coach House had been transformed into a restaurant and tea garden. The excellent tea was most welcome. Sitting in the grounds looking at the manicured gardens and sipping from the bone china cups and savouring floury scones served on a fine compote, one could imagine that Juliet and her cousin, Edward Knatchbull, would come strolling arm in arm through the rose arbour at any second.*

The Hatch still belongs to the Knatchbulls. Patricia Knatchbull, Lady Mountbatten of Burma, died in the June of 2017 and her funeral reception was held there.

The sorrow, and sense of loss at finishing this work, is mitigated somewhat by the knowledge that I can always pop into Edward Knatchbull's place for afternoon tea, or visit any of the mediaeval churches in the area, to feel close to the strong personalities that inspired this book. I hope your enjoyment in reading it matches mine in writing it.

Lyn Watts – December 2017

The Bourne Tap

So be easy and free, when you're drinkin' wi me,
I'm a man you don't meet every day.'
(Scottish traditional song, Jock Stewart)

George sat outside in his garden. He liked to sit quietly on his horse and watch the world go by while Bet entertained inside. She loved a party. A big, buxom, jolly woman, she loved her gin and a singsong.

George was more sedate. He preferred to keep a clear head and a professional working relationship with the men that Bet was entertaining within the walls of their home. Never one for drinking, George preferred to let her run the show inside their cottage which, on some nights, became a tap bar selling unlicensed liquor. This was where Geneva, ale and brandy flowed; dancing, and, he had no doubt, general debauchery took place. He had built the cottage as a means of

2

selling some of his goods, free traded from France. Sometimes people would come from over thirty miles away with horse and cart to carry away the tubs George supplied. Bought for just £1 in France they sold for £4 each from George in England. This was a little over £1 a gallon rather than the usual price of over two pounds five shillings. George sometimes sold more than a hundred a week. The parties in the Bourne Tap, their home, were Bets way of selling the liquor and tobacco plus making a shilling or two back from the generous wages paid to the men George employed on his runs.

George would sit outside during these evenings, either on his bench or astride his favourite horse, smoking a pipe and, no doubt, planning his next run to France. If the weather was inclement, he would retreat into the cart lodge, and watch the world go by from comparative dryness.

Not much happened in that part of the countryside. Aldington village itself was busy, but here it was desolate woodland or common land and about a mile and a half outside of the Kentish village. That was exactly why George liked it and why he had built the cottage in the first place. It was ideally suited for the roads to Ashford and the coast, but away from prying eyes.

Of course, according to the nosey villagers, it was all that was evil and a hotbed of sin. They said that all kinds of depravity and debauchery happened here. They called the area Aldington Fright! It was officially named Aldington Frith, which means a peaceful wooded area! George encouraged these tales. It instilled a certain element of fear and largely kept unwanted folk away.

The villagers didn't complain to outsiders because there was hardly a one of them that didn't benefit, or have a better lifestyle, thanks to George's business enterprises. He always paid his men in advance; eight shillings for tub carriers, twenty shillings for batsmen. That was more than a week's wages for most of them. George was known locally as 'Captain Bats' after the oak cudgels his men carried to protect themselves. There was always the threat of arrest by the coastal blockade force, when out on a run. These batsmen would form a circle around the tubmen facing out with their bats ready to beat off any attacking revenue men. The tubs were all roped together and the tubmen had to work like lightening cutting the ropes with very sharp knives to separate them for transport. Even a small lack of concentration could cost a finger or, at the very least, a deeply cut hand!

Born at Ruckinge Kent, George began his working life as a carter and a ploughman at Court Lodge Farm which was a short distance away. A very good carter and horseman he was too, by all accounts

Rumour had it that he had once found a stash of spirits buried in a field. He sold them all, which enabled him to buy the cottage now known as the Bourne Tap. He liked its location, and the fact that it was ideally placed as a 'blind pig' to sell his illicit goods.

By 1822 George Ransley had become the leader of the Aldington Blues. They were a gang of smugglers, or free traders as they were known. At that time their official meeting place was the Walnut Tree Inn in the village. It was where the landings and the strategy of the runs were worked out. The snug back room and attic look-out were perfect for the gang to see and signal across the marshes.

George stayed sober. His quick brain and eye for business needed to be clear and uncluttered by strong drink. It had been the downfall of his predecessor, Cephas Quested, who now lay in an unmarked grave in Aldington churchyard.

Cephas had been a big, jolly, blustering man. He was kindly but not possessed of the sharpest intellect! He had led the gang on their nocturnal runs, but would tap the very tubs on his back for a drink. Indeed that had been his downfall. It was reported that, at one time, he and a man called Gardiner, had tapped the tubs and drunk themselves into a stupor. They lay down and slept outdoors all night. It was a freezing cold winter's night. In the morning a farmer found them. Gardiner was dead from exposure. On being told the news Cephas is reported to have said "Well, he died of what he loved!"

The gang had run a cargo at Camber on the 11th of February 1821. They were spotted on the beach by the blockade sentries who fired several warning shots to the patrols in the vicinity. They were pursued inland by the blockaders led by young Midshipman McKenzie who caught up with them at Brookland, on the Walland Marsh. A huge and bloody battle ensued with volley after volley fired into the smugglers ranks and many a cutlass charge made. At the end McKenzie lay dead, shot in the chest, and two blockade officers plus six of their men were wounded.

The Blues lost four dead and had sixteen wounded. After the fighting was over a very drunken Cephas was found flat on his back in a reed bed, asleep. On being woken, he had handed the man who had wakened him his pistol and told him to: "Blow a bloody officers brains out!"

Unfortunately for Cephas that man was a revenue officer! Cephas had mistaken his blue jacket for one of the gang's blue smocks. He was tried at Newgate and sentenced to hang in chains. Whilst he was in prison he was forced to remain sober. Surprisingly, he found that he quite liked the life. He learnt to say the Lord's Prayer, and he carved a little wooden snuff box in the shape of a shoe to give to his wife. Shortly before his execution, he told his wife: "We eat and drink today Pat, and tomorrow we die."

He was quite prepared to meet his fate. George himself had persuaded the Squire, Edward Knatchbull, local magistrate and MP (who was also a beneficiary of the gang's illicit goods) to intervene. The sentence was commuted to just hanging. He was hung on the 4th of July 1821. His wife Martha, whom he always called Pat, was allowed to bring the body home to Aldington.

Cephas lay in state in his cottage for the night before his burial and all of the villagers came to pay their respects. Martha coped very well. He was buried on July the 8th 1821, the burial performed by John Hollams, curate. Cephas was 32 years old.

The little wooden snuff box was destined to end up in Ashford museum sometime in the future, in the very building that was designed as the local school, built by the generosity of Sir Norton Knatchbull, Sir Edward's son.

After the death of Cephas, his brother James Quested stayed as a member of the gang and went on most of their runs with them. The Battle of Brookland, as it became known, was a brief setback. The gang had to be more subtle with their operations for a while but they were clearly not deterred.

Cephas could have turned King's Evidence against the gang and saved himself, but he would not. He was kept in prison and his execution was delayed for longer than was usual. This was in the hope that he would betray his friends and save himself. "No," he told them

"I've done wrong and I will pay for it, but I won't bring harm upon others."

Poor Cephas; when George heard of this he repaid him by ensuring that Martha and their surviving children were well catered for financially (until she remarried shortly after Cephas' death.) George himself vowed that he would not make the same mistake as Cephas.

****

George could hear Bet's raucous laughter ring out. It fair set the cups rattling on the dresser! It set his teeth on edge at times too! For that reason he felt that he had to get out. Betsy, or Elizabeth Bailey to give her full name, was the daughter of another smuggler. Samuel Bailey, known as Thresher Bailey for his habit of carrying a threshing flail on the runs, was her father. The flail was there to be used on any pursuers heads if needs be! The Bailey's were a famous smuggling family in that part of Kent. Bet's father and brothers were all members of the Blues.

George loved Bet - indeed, they had ten children (nine of whom survived). They had been married on St Valentine's Day 1809 in St Rumwold's church at Bonnington. He often wondered if he would have married at all had she not been four months pregnant with their first born, Matilda. Yes, he loved her, but she was loud; loud, brash and sometimes too much for his fastidious taste.

The back door of the cottage swung open bringing with it a burst of noise and a strong smell of sweat, tobacco and brandy. The two Wire brothers staggered out into the garden laughing. Richard, Dick to his friends, the older brother found a tree to relieve himself behind while little William spat out the quid of tobacco he had been chewing and opened his smock at the neck to cool down.

Suddenly he paused, ear cocked towards the road. George could hear it too; hoof beats and wheels rattling on the stony ground. Very few people travelled this way, so they were surprised when into view came a small two wheeled Tilbury gig pulled by a fine grey horse and driven, rather well, by Juliet Knatchbull, widow of Major James Knatchbull, late cousin to the local MP and squire.

George had always admired Juliet. In her thirties still, she had been widowed when her only son was still in swaddling. Her husband had been killed, along with half his regiment, at Waterloo. She had maintained the modest double-fronted house in the village with only an elderly manservant and a general maid. She was popular with the locals; generous with her time and always willing to help anyone less fortunate than herself. Samuel Knatchbull, her son, was away at school, so she had thrown herself into undertaking good works around the village. Better still, George liked her looks. She was an attractive woman, neat and trim with chestnut hair and bright green eyes. She was also very intelligent.

He wondered what she was doing at this hour, past seven in the evening, driving through this part of the area alone; more than a little risky, he thought.

Just as he was musing, Dick came staggering around from the tree buttoning up his breeches. Will nudged his brother and nodded towards the road where Juliet was driving towards them.

They stepped out in front of her, giving her no option but to stop. Young Will spoke to her: "Evening Ma'am, nice eve for a drive ain't it?"

As he spoke Dick sidled up to the cart and took her basket, empty now, from the seat next to her. She stiffened. "Yes," she said "a nice evening, may I pass through please. It's late and I need to get back." She looked nervous and eyed Dick as he took her basket.
"Well, ain't much in 'ere!" He said, "What you gonna pay the toll with then? I know! A kiss! The toll is one kiss apiece to pass!" and he placed his hand on her knee.

"Alright you two, that's enough of that" said George riding from the darkness of the shaw by the garden. He swung his short riding whip at Richard who leapt back with shock. "Get out! I won't have this on my watch! Go home and don't come back to me until you are sober and have learnt some manners." His voice was low and sounded menacing. "Now apologise to Mrs Knatchbull." "Yes, Captain! Sorry, Captain!" The brothers looked ashamed. "Sorry Ma'am, no harm intended!" Then they scuttled off rapidly with sullen looks on their faces.

George turned towards Juliet: "I do apologise for their manners Ma'am." "Thank you, Mr Ransley, it was not your fault. Thank you for intervening when you did." She had looked very worried but now her face showed a mixture of relief and gratitude. George softened his voice: "Not a good idea to be driving alone in this area at this hour anyway, Ma'am. It is not the safest of areas at dusk."

"Old Mrs Rook at Mersham is gravely ill. Her son is still unable to work until his leg heals since his thatching accident. I take them a basket of provisions every week to help them out. This time it grew later than I realised. If I drive the main road way it is three miles further. This is a short cut, I…. I never thought … I never believe any rumours I hear anyway…" At this point she broke off and blushed.

"May I ride with you?" asked George softly: "See you safely home like?" Juliet nodded her consent.

George rode next to her. He relished her intelligent conversation. He enjoyed the faint waft of her expensive perfume, her lovely face. Bet wouldn't even miss him. By the time he got back she would more than likely be sleeping off her gin induced partying.

Juliet discovered that George had a quick intellect and was an amazingly knowledgeable horseman. He told her of his life as a carter at Court Lodge Farm in Aldington. He hinted at his skill as a free trader. It was known that it had benefitted both his family and many a local family around. She learned that he had mainly kept out of trouble, only stealing corn on a few occasions to feed his beloved horses. The farmer had forgiven this with little persuasion as he valued his skills with the horses.

George had found some monies from somewhere. There was a rumour that he had found a stash of smuggled spirits hidden, sold them on and gave up working. He was a little cagey on that one, she felt. He had built the Bourne Tap with the profit from their sales, so the rumour went on, and devoted himself full time to the "Free Trade". It was said that his runs increased the average household income by 100% for many of his men. The profit on some of his goods was as high as 600%. Indeed, Juliet knew for a fact that her cousin, Squire Knatchbull, had enjoyed many a pipe and bumper of Geneva from the Blues' runs.

Captain Bats he was called in the village. She suspected why! It was said that he could be as ruthless as the situation demanded, but, this evening, Juliet saw a very different side to his character. He was charming, polite and gentle. She found him surprisingly intelligent for a carter.

Eventually Laurel House came into view and she was home. George insisted on taking her horse into its stable himself, leaving her manservant, Josh, to deal with the harness.

"May I offer you refreshment before your return journey?" she asked. George declined. He just accepted water for his horse before remounting.

"Can I meet you next week and ride with you?" he asked. Juliet nodded her consent then, reddening, she turned to go in as George doffed his hat and wheeled his horse around before cantering off up towards the Frith road.

"Well?" She demanded of little Jane, her maid, who had been staring open mouthed. The girl executed a swift bob then lifted her skirts and flitted up the stairs to light the bedroom fires.

The Ransley grave board, Ruckinge church

The Roaring Ransleys

'A dreadful sight there is to see
Two brothers hanging from a tree;
A shocking sight for to behold-
The Lord have mercy on our souls.'
(from a song printed and hawked at the Ransley brothers execution)

So that was George Ransley. Of course Juliet had seen him; knew who he was; saw him about the village, the church and such, but she had never before spoken to him. Rumour said all manner of things about him. She had half expected a savage, child eating primitive, yet surely he couldn't be so successful at his trade if that were true.

She had found him dashing, intelligent and well mannered. In his mid- forties, he had a pleasant, attractive face, brown hair and blue eyes. He was of average height and stocky; possessing great muscular strength. He had a ready smile and was softly spoken. He

14

intrigued her, for he had a double row of teeth in his top jaw, giving a rather odd, but attractive, appearance to his smile. How fortunate he had come along when he had. Those Wire boys had worried her. She sighed. Sleep eluded her tonight. She must put him out of her mind. Turning her pillow she tried to compose her mind for sleep; but she looked forward to next week's trip home from Mrs Rook's nonetheless.

George cantered towards the Frith road. He thought what a charming woman Juliet Knatchbull was. She was capable and independent, intelligent and yet had a certain vulnerability about her. His father would have called her "above their station in life". George knew instinctively that Juliet held no store by a man's class; more by what sort of a man he was and judged by how he treated his fellow man, or woman. Her cousin, Edward, up at Mersham Hatch, was a Tory MP but the Knatchbull's were known to have liberal views and to be local benefactors.

The Ransleys hadn't always had a good reputation locally. Known as The Roaring Ransleys, they had, in the past, been feared by the locals. George had changed all that, yet only twenty five years back in history the local area had been plagued by his two elder cousins.

William and James Ransley were a bad lot. Known locally as The Rascally Brothers, they were horse thieves, robbers and ruffians.

They now both lay in Ruckinge churchyard - the Ransley grave marked by a simple wooden grave board. Aged just 25 and 23, they had become too cock-sure of themselves. They had a history of theft, assault and extortion. James had been in trouble for stealing and housebreaking. William had served three months in prison for assaulting one Ann Wilson who was the landlady of the Blue Anchor public house. Eventually they stole one horse too many in a drunken rage and the law had caught up with them. They were tried in Maidstone with the offence of common burglary, found guilty and subsequently hung at Penenden Heath in August 1800. George's Uncle, their father, had been in person with a cart to collect their corpses and bring them home. Such was the reputation of the family that, as their father, James Byham Ransley, set off on his sorrowful journey, an old village woman shouted from her porch "Don't forgit to bring some sugar back with ye as well as the corpses, Mr Ransley".

There were several hung on that day at Penenden Heath. Isaac Ballard swung for highway robbery. He had been at one time the landlord of the Blue Anchor. The other, a Robert Radford, was hung for the rape of Susannah Clinton who was aged just eight years. Strangely enough the offence was committed right outside the Blue Anchor!

The rest of the brother's family moved to Mersham. Seven years after the hangings, in 1807, their sister, Elizabeth, her mind disturbed by the manner of her brothers' death, hung herself in her bedroom. She was just twenty-two years old.

Young John, the only surviving son was a mere eight year old when his brothers were hung. George himself was ten years older than that, but it had made an impression. Don't get caught was George's philosophy, whereas John vowed to always lead an honest life. The death of his older brothers, and then the suicide of his sister, had affected him very deeply. Refusing to have anything to do with illicit goods, or anything remotely on the wrong side of the law, he ran the family farm and sold his wool legitimately. George liked and respected him even though he lacked the daring that George himself had.

One reason George had employed the Wire brothers, was that they reminded him of his two errant cousins. The Wire brothers had lost their father when just 18 and 15 years old. He had been struck by lightning whilst working in the fields. This was in August 1823. He was still holding the metal fork when the blast hit him. He died instantly. Their mother and his elder brother, Thomas, managed their 30 acre holding at Aldington with precious little help from the younger siblings. George had a vague idea that he might try to exert some paternal influence over the two brothers, but, God knew, it was an uphill struggle.

****

George had a run organised from Dover the next evening. Since the service had started in 1820, he would take the steam packet over to France and buy a boat there. He would then organise his crew, mainly from Folkestone, to sail back with tubs of brandy and Geneva to a pre-arranged place and at a pre-arranged time. He would have up to 200 tubs, each holding about three and a quarter gallons. It was frantically busy at these times. He had over eighty men to muster and organise for each run; but he would look forward to seeing Juliet Knatchbull safely home the next week come what may.

Most times, when there was a run to organise, George would call a meeting of the core members of the gang to discuss the logistics of it all. The Walnut Tree Inn in Aldington was the ideal place to hold these meetings. A quiet back room gave them the privacy they needed to discuss their business without being overheard. If they were waiting for cargo to be brought in a small room, accessed by a ladder, had a high side window from which their signal, made by a flashing lamp, could be seen for many miles by those awaiting it. The landlord benefitted from the gang's uncustomed goods too, and sold some of it back to them on such evenings as these.

The Blues only organised and executed about half a dozen runs every year. In the first place George had to go over to France to purchase the goods. The next stage was the arrangement to ship the goods over to a chosen quiet bay or beach on a pre-arranged date. Once the boats had arrived without mishap the goods had to be unloaded and then hidden away safely. The distribution of the cargo had to be carried out to pre-found customers. After that the next run's customers and suppliers needed to be found. The tubmen and the batsmen needed to be recruited and put on stand-by for the next time they would be needed. It was a fact that every time any of the gang went on a run they risked their lives. This was not only from the excise officers, armed with a brace of pistols and a cutlass each, but also from His Majesty's government. The gangs' activities carried a death sentence should they be caught and found guilty

The profit was between 300 and a 600% on each successful run. There was not the need for very many in order to grow rich.

****

The following week George met Juliet on the road just outside Mersham, a couple of hundred yards from the Rook's cottage. They rode and drove slowly, relishing the warm early spring evening and the conversation, which was different to any either of them usually had in their respective social circles. He liked the way the evening sun made her chestnut hair gleam. For her part it had been ages since such a fine looking man had given her this much attention. Before they knew it Laurel House came into view and, after settling her horse and watering his own, George said his farewells to Juliet and rode home.

This continued for the next two weeks, but, on the third week, George accepted Juliet's offer of refreshment. He sat opposite her by the fire and drank a glass of Madeira while they talked. They never seemed to be short of conversation. On taking his leave he gently kissed the back of her hand and bowed, his lips lingering longer than was customary and their eyes meeting briefly before Juliet looked away blushing. George mounted his horse while Juliet was still blushing as she turned into the house. The following day he was driving his own horses to his cousin's farm when he heard the bell of St John the Baptist's church in Mersham tolling.

John poured him a small ale and told him that old Mrs Rook had finally succumbed to her illness and had gone to meet her maker. A deep anxiety gripped George's heart. What now? Juliet would no longer need to visit the cottage at Mersham. In an act typical of the woman, she had petitioned her cousin, Squire Knatchbull, to give Francis Rook a position as an under gardener on his estate since his leg injury rendered impossible the climbing of roofs for thatching. This signified no more trips to the cottage and no more rides home together. He was surprised at how much it troubled him.

Juliet was sorry to hear of the passing of Mrs Rook. She felt a greater sorrow at losing her weekly trips home with George Ransley.

Since losing her husband she had busied herself with Samuel, her son. Her charitable works had consumed most of the remainder of her time and she had not had much opportunity for mixing with members of the opposite sex, let alone enjoying such stimulating conversation. George had opened up a whole new and exciting world to her. A world of daring exploits, moonlight trips across to the continent, and of staying one step ahead of the excise men.

He was a fascinating person. Juliet had never met a totally self- made man before. Most of her social circle were gentry. They were well educated people who accepted their privileges in life as their God given right. George was resourceful and intelligent, compassionate, yet, she believed, ruthless if the situation demanded it. He had succeeded in life by his wit and charm. His smuggling and the Bourne Tap enabled him to give up employment and work full time at the free trade. George's intellect had been wasted as a mere carter but it was true to say that he did have a great love and a huge knowledge of horses. Juliet was impressed with the gentleness and patience which he showed to the animals in his care. She always judged a person's character by the way they treated those more vulnerable than themselves. His eye for business and his way with people meant he had quickly risen through the ranks of the Blues to become their leader following the capture of Cephas Quested. She thought him a great leader of men.

George employed the gangs' own doctor, one Ralph Hougham of Pear Tree House, Brookland. The good doctor would often be led blindfolded to his casualties so that he could treat members of both sides - revenue men too - without compromising either his, or the gang's, safety.

Ralph Pepworth Hougham was born in 1785 to a fairly high-class wealthy family. His Grandfather had been a fairly prominent English architect. He had married Ann Parkins in 1809. She was some five years his senior. By her he had sixteen children, nine of whom survived. In 1815 they moved from Lydd to Brookland. By that time Ralph was so reduced in fortune, probably from keeping his large family, that he was shoeless and had to borrow a shirt so that his could be washed. George had changed all that for him, keeping him in his employ. That, coupled with his village practice, increased his fortunes. In return he was loyal to the gang. He had a red Moroccan leather wallet made in which he kept all his instruments and medicines to take with him when he treated the injured. It fitted secretly into the pocket of his greatcoat.

George looked after the families of those gang members killed or injured in the affrays with the revenue officers. Martha Quested and her children wanted for nothing, after Cephas' death until she became another man's responsibility. George employed two expensive, top, Ashford solicitors, Messrs Langham and Platt, to fight for the gang members in any court cases they might be caught up in. This ensured the loyalty of their families and, as a consequence, the whole village was on his side.

George's eldest son managed his books for him and helped out on the runs. George owned a boat and he employed experienced sailors to crew it for him on the trips. They would often rope the tubs and attach sinkers to them. That way, if their operations were interrupted by revenue officers, they could drop them over the side to be retrieved later with grappling irons. These boats were made in France by boat builders imported into the country mainly from Folkestone and Dover. It was easier to produce small boats in France to avoid the heavy taxes imposed by the British Government to discourage smugglers. They were fairly cheap at around £40 each compared to the profits of about £450 made on each run. If disturbed by blockaders, it was cheaper to sink the tubs (to be retrieved later) and scupper the boat. A new one could easily be purchased from the night's profit. The location of the tubs could be marked by a subtle floating marker, sometimes something as inconspicuous as a gulls feather bobbing on the sea surface.

It was little wonder that he inspired great loyalty in his men. He knew just which type of man was needed for each job. Sadly, sometimes, that meant employing ruffians like the Wire brothers.

****

Two weeks passed after Mrs Rook's funeral. Despite her best efforts to put him out of her head Juliet found her mind continually wandering onto George Ransley. She knew it was wrong. He was a married man with a large family, but she couldn't help her thoughts continually drifting back to him.

As for George, she filled his mind constantly. He loved Bet, but was totally infatuated with Juliet. He missed her grace, her conversation and her wit. He would sit outside on his horse for hours in the hope that she might come past just once.

One dark Saturday night there was a terrific storm; so fierce was the wind and rain that any chance of a cargo being landed that night was scuppered. The usual raucous orgy was taking place in the Bourne Tap.

In Laurel House Juliet had sent Jane, her maid, to bed. The girl was only fifteen and worked quite hard enough; an early night would do her good. The old manservant, Josh, slept in the bothy above the stables.

Juliet sat alone by the fire. She knew that with the noise of the storm raging outside that sleep would be impossible. She went to the window and looked out onto the street to see if the storm showed any sign of abating. The trees opposite swayed and rustled in the wind, just visible against the weak, watery moon. A flash of forked lightening suddenly illuminated a familiar figure standing opposite the house in the rain. George was staring at Juliet's window. He had tipped his tall hat forward to keep the rain out of his eyes. He was leaning against a tree with one booted leg bent up at the knee and his arms folded. Juliet put her candle on the window ledge and stepped back from the window. A clap of thunder, then a tap on the door; the figure opposite had disappeared. Juliet drew back the pin and opened the door a little. George stood there streaming water. She stood aside and he strode in. she hardly had time to close and bolt the door, before he threw his hat aside and had her in his arms.

Their kiss was passionate and went on and on. She felt a long supressed tingle as his body pressed against her through his wet clothes. They had both waited a long time for this moment, so had no desire to rush it. They only broke off kissing for her to grab his hand and the candle to lead him upstairs.

As Juliet kicked the bedroom door closed behind them, Jane drew back from her hidden viewpoint at the top of the attic stairs, her eyes like saucers. 'So the Missus loves old Captain Bats!' she thought. 'Disgusting at their ages, why, she is in her thirties and he must be forty if he's a day. Old people are strange the way they carry on!' She blew out her candle.

The Walnut Tree Inn, Aldington

The Blues

'The King he is a proud man, in his grand red coat
But I do love a Smuggler, in his little fishing boat,
For he runs the Mallins Lace, and he spends his money free
And I would I were a sailor, to go along with he!'
Traditional West Country smuggling song

The gang had a run booked at Sandgate. The cargo had been scheduled to land at Deal three nights previously but the signal had been received that the blockaders were about on the beach so the run had been abandoned and the boat returned to France to await George's further instructions.

Juliet was keen to see George. She knew he would never be hers completely, that they could never be truly together, but she lived for their secret liaisons. After the night of the storm he had regularly called and stayed the night. She was keen to hear how the landing at Sandgate had gone as she constantly feared that the coastal blockade would catch up with George and his men.

He arrived the following evening, sometime after midnight. As they lay in bed he told her about the run. She loved those times when, at post coital peace, she would lie with her head on his chest and he would stroke her hair and tell her of his latest exploits.

George told her about the aborted run they had had on 5th April at No 27 Tower, near Hythe. At around 9 in the evening they were about to work the cargo when they were fired on by a small party of blockaders led by Admiralty Mate Eugene O'Reilly. Under steady fire, with several of them wounded, the Gang had no choice but to "flash" off the boat to prevent it landing and retreat up the beach. This was the firing of the warning blue flares. They were followed a considerable way inland by the blockade party, who only ceased firing at them when George's batsmen, the two big Bailey men, and Dutchy (Thomas) Gilham, beat the nearest ones off with heavy and debilitating blows.

There was a bizarre outcome of this affray in that the blockaders accidently shot and killed one of their own men. Hearing distant firing, a sentinel called Lemon, near Fort Twiss, thought they were about to be attacked and started firing his pistols. Lieutenant Dyer received four gun-shot wounds to the upper part of his body which proved fatal. "They save us a lot of work, finishing each other off!" joked George to Juliet.

It had been a near thing on the Sandgate run. The blockade had been close by and one officer, a landsman, had seen them and tried to fire off a warning flare to his colleagues. George, James Smeed and Bet's brother Samuel Bailey had overpowered him before he could send the alarm. Binding his legs and blindfolding him they told him he was to be thrown off one of the high cliffs. They purposely left his hands free to clutch at some tufts of grass at the cliff edge as they slowly rolled him over. Leaving him dangling there, they easily made their escape. The poor man hung on as long as he could, but his hands grew numb and his arms were agonisingly painful. The grass was tearing away from the top when he could grip no longer. He let go and prepared to die.

Plop! He landed on his feet not more than 18 inches from the ground. At no time had he been in any real danger, the Blues had left him on one of the small chalk pits no more than 7 foot high!

Juliet's face went from registering shock and disgust to high amusement on hearing the fate of the man! She shook with laughter and teased him in mock horror: "Oh Mr Ransley, you are incorrigible!" pretending to be scandalised. "I love making you laugh." He told her, "I love you anyway." and with that he rolled over and kissed her again.

Some weeks later Juliet had to visit a family in Bilsington, just a mile or two outside Aldington. There was an ancient Augustinian priory there, at that time it was used as a farmhouse. Juliet was curious about it as she had heard rumours that it was haunted by a severed head – as a re-enactment of an historical murder. Not believing these rumours for a second, she was yet curious to know why they had been started in the first place.

As she drove her horse along the lanes she mused on this. The building hove into view. It was a weathered, mellow stone building, quite isolated and looked a little forlorn - as most of those old priories did following the dissolution. As she passed by slowly, looking at the building, she heard men's voices. Out of the side of the building, coming down the path was George with some other men!

His face lit up when he saw her, but he said in a formal fashion: "Good morning Mrs Knatchbull, I trust the morning finds you well?" His blue eyes twinkled. Juliet, blushed, but quickly recovering from her surprise she replied equally formally that she was well, thanked him for asking, then wished him good day and continued on her way.

Juliet had a quick intellect. It didn't take her more than a few seconds to work out why the rumours had been circulated. If George Ransley and his men were using the priory to store their contraband, then such stories would keep prying eyes away.

The gang used a variety of places to store their free traded goods. Some were offered happily, others were reluctantly granted by their owners through fear of reprisals; the loss of livestock or the odd haystack fire, for example. These latter were in the minority though, as most of the local population benefitted from the trade. St George's church at Ivychurch was just such a place, as was St Dunstan's at Snargate, St Earnswith at Brenzett and St Thomas a Beckett at Fairfield. The latter being ideal as it was only accessible by boat at high tide across a small stream and marshy fields.

The Rector's and parsons were compliant with this as many of them benefitted from the odd tub of brandy or pipe of tobacco. The lead font at St Augustine's Brookland had been used to hide contraband from time to time. At St George's Ivychurch, the Rector, George Gleig, was an absentee. A Scottish soldier now retired from army life, he took the living at Ivychurch, and promptly announced that the rectory was too damp and the marsh miasmas were making him ill! So he lived in London. From there he could write all his books and works for Blackwood's magazine, mostly on military matters. This meant that other local curates would sometimes come and take such services as there were, but, for the most part, the smugglers had free run of the church and the crypt.

Sometimes the church would be closed for days at a time. Usually following a run from the continent, a sign would be hung on the door reading "No services until further notice." Rumour had it that there was a tunnel leading from St George's crypt on the south aisle to the cellar of the Bell public house next door. Customers had often reported strange noises coming from underneath the pub on some evenings.

The Reverend Richard Harris Barham, who was also a writer, lived at the Vicarage at St Dunstan's Snargate. Indeed some years later Juliet believed his work, The Ingoldsby Legends, to have been inspired by the Aldington Gang's exploits. He often told Edward Knatchbull, her cousin, that he could find his way home across the marshes simply by following the pungent waft of tobacco and brandy emanating from his church crypt! One dark winter's night he was riding home carefully across Walland Marsh when he spotted a line of ponies and a large group of men, all walking silently. The men were armed with oaken cudgels and carried spout lanterns while the ponies all had double packs strung across their backs. His feeling of unease quickly passed when the lead man called out to the others: "Why, it's alright lads, 'tis only the Parson!" then "Evening Vicar!" They all muttered a greeting as they passed him and the last man handed him a tub of finest Geneva with a wink!

Mersham Hatch

Cousins

'Friendship is the only cement that will ever hold the Cousins together'
Woodrow Wilson

Now it happened that Juliet was visiting her cousin Edward at Mersham. Although they were only cousins by marriage, Edward was fond of Juliet and her little boy. He had promised her late husband, before he left with his regiment for war, that he would always look out for them and they would want for nothing. Indeed, he and Juliet had a mutual understanding of grief. He had lost his first wife in childbirth in 1814, a year before Juliet lost James.

Edward Knatchbull had happily remarried, some six years previously, a charming lady called Fanny whom Juliet got on very well with. Edward was a local magistrate and held the Tory seat as member for Kent. He had inherited the Baronetcy on the death of his father and now ran his vast estates and country house, the Hatch, at Mersham, some 2 miles from Aldington.

Juliet was always pleased to see her cousin. She pulled up outside his house and handed the reins of her pony and carriage to Edward's groom. Running past the maid who opened the front door, she ran into Edwards study with a gleeful cry of: "Hello you old bear!" then stopped short and blushed as she came face to face with a strange, yet familiar looking man.

John Ransley had a few acres of his own at his home, Ransley House, in Kingsford Street, Mersham. He had inherited the family home. It was set in a most desolate lonely spot; indeed, the only neighbour was the local Union (what we would know today as the Workhouse). He lived there with his children and Sarah, one of his unmarried sisters, since the death of his wife some four years previously. Determined to remain on the right side of the law following the execution of his two elder brothers, he made his living by farming. His own lands being inadequately small, he also rented several acres from Edward. Today he had come to pay his tithes.

"Oh I'm sorry! I.. I.." but Edward, grinning, cut her short "Serves you right, cousin! Mr Ransley, this is my cousin Mrs James Knatchbull." then looking at Juliet: "This is Mr John Ransley".

Juliet was surprised at how much he resembled his own cousin. He was obviously some years younger, but he had the same piercing blue eyes and brown hair as George. If anything his hair was even more luxuriant. He was a few inches taller too and had a different kind of smile as his teeth were evenly set, but it was a very attractive smile nonetheless.

John gave a slight bow and Juliet executed a brief bob. "Do excuse me, Mrs Knatchbull; Sir Edward I wish you good morning." He nodded towards Edward and doffed his hat as he took his leave.

Edward was amused at Juliet. His eyes scanned her face and she felt herself blush. Did he know about her and George she wondered? How could he know? And yet she felt guilty all the same.

Juliet saw George every few days. Sometimes it would only be a fleeting visit when he had pressing business matters to attend to; so he would drop by, they would talk and occasionally share a glass or two. At other times he would stay over and they would enjoy a night of desperate passion that never waned. No matter which, George was always generous and loving. He regularly brought gifts for her; sometimes fine laces, Madeira wine or perfumes, sometimes just a single flower. Juliet told him about her embarrassing meeting with his cousin John. George was fond of John. They had become close following the execution of his two older brothers and John looked to George for advice and guidance on matters from time to time.

Juliet felt some empathy for him, especially since he looked like a younger version of her George.

George was highly amused at her embarrassment on the nature of their meeting and teased her. He wasn't a bit concerned at what others thought. Whenever Juliet felt guilt about their relationship he would hug her and say "Don't worry Jules, we're in good company, why even the King has his Mrs Fitzherbert!"

Whilst she knew it was wrong, and he could never truly be hers, Juliet couldn't help herself. She loved him. Jane her maid had come to accept the situation and never mentioned it. George sometimes brought some French ribbons or trinkets for her. Juliet knew that old Josh must know what was going on, but he got on very well with George as they had their mutual love of horses in common, and he too would receive the odd tub of brandy to keep out the cold. Her servants were both very loyal to her so she had no fears of either of them giving their secret away.

George felt some slight guilt about Bet. She was a good woman for all her faults; but she had her pleasures - her house and gin and, above all, her partying. Juliet was his pleasure and he did love them both, he just needed to make sure neither one of them suffered by the situation.

At that moment in time he had enough problems. Some of the younger gang members had acquired duck guns and small flintlock pistols. George had always employed batsmen - the men who carried the long oaken cudgels or "bats" on the runs as a protection from the blockaders - but the taking up of arms, well, that was a different matter.

Some of the older members wanted out. As one older smuggler said to George: "Cheating the Government is one thing as the Government, well, he cheats you; but the taking up of arms against King and Country, well, that's plain wrong!" George was inclined to agree.

In the December of the previous year, 1825, a gang member from East Kent had been killed by a blockade officer called Richard Morgan on the beach at Dymchurch. Morgan was midshipman on HMS Ramillies and was leading a patrol on the beach.

They had sent a landing party (including Richard) in a small boat. Charles Keely and his party were on the shore unloading. Keely eyed the man standing at the boat's helm: "We can take him from here!" he hissed to his colleagues.

A pistol was fired at the boat. The bullet whizzed past the seaman at the helm, grazing his right cheek. He yelped in pain and surprise.

Richard Morgan pulled out his pistol and fired at the sniper - in the dark he could only make out shapes. His pistol failed to fire. A musket was aimed at him in return. The trigger was pulled by one of the gang. By some miracle the musket flashed in the pan, to the accompaniment of much cussing by the smuggler. This gave Richard valuable seconds to retrieve his second pistol from his belt, aim to where he had seen the flash and fire. He saw the silhouette of the sniper lurch back as the bullet hit him full in the chest. The victim staggered, fell to his knees, then pitched face downward onto the sand. He saw the other gang members drop their booty and flee! They had left the contraband, and their dead colleague, behind. Richard, and his fellow seaman, ran the last few yards through the shallow water to the beach. They turned the dead man onto his back. It was Charles Keely. Keely now lay at rest in the Churchyard of St Peter and St Paul at Dymchurch.

The gang were out for revenge on Morgan, but guns were not the way, thought George. Keely was proof of that.

Murder on Dover Beach

'Stay, reader, stay, incline your ear
To know who this is buried here
A husband dear, a brother kind,
A friend to all the well inclined'
Richard Morgan's epitaph

The months wore on and for Juliet life was exciting. She loved her time with George. She had fallen for him in a big way, and yet she knew they could never be together. For his part she was his inspiration. He felt capable of anything with the love of a woman like her behind him. He really did love both of the women in his life. He knew the situation could never last though.

Juliet was worried for his safety. On 11th May, about 150 smugglers had converged on the coast at Herring Hang near Hythe. Charles Giles, one of the gang's inner circle, had been shot in the neck. He was one of a group of armed men who had fired at a party of preventative service men and marines. They had been stationed at Herring Hang to disrupt the smuggling activity. The seamen seized a long duck gun that had been left behind. This possibly belonged to Charles since he is reported to have lost his firearm on that occasion. George ordered Edward Horne to carry Giles to a small green field some forty or fifty yards from the action. With Giles able to walk a little, they made their way to the high road where George collected Giles in his cart. He was then taken to West Wall, beyond Ashford, where an aunt was able to take care of him while the flesh wound to his neck healed enough to be passed off as the effects of a blister. Dr Beet from Ashford attended him - paid for by George - and said he was lucky. It could have been so much worse.

George always said that after Giles had been shot, all of the scouts were afraid of the blockaders with the exceptions of John Bailey, James Smeed and Dutchy. This was the nickname they used for Thomas Gilham as his alias was Datchet Grey.

Local support for the gang was beginning to wane. By the summer of 1826 the younger members of the gang had become too full of themselves and larky. Flushed with their own success, they would take pot shots at cattle in the fields on their way home from a run. They would also charge through the villages shouting and firing their pistols into the air, disrupting the peace. They broke into houses and began robbing the villagers. One night they charged through Aldington and broke into the Walnut Tree inn, stripping it bare of all pies, puddings, cakes and anything edible. George felt he had to recompense the landlord for that. He was beginning to lose control of them and told Juliet that he felt that local sympathy was draining away.

On 30th July 1826, about one in the morning, Richard Morgan and the coastal blockade were on duty on Dover Beach. They observed a boat in the surf, heavily laden with tubs of spirits. The crew, with the assistance of some of the gang, attempted to run the cargo. One of the blockaders ordered them to surrender and was roundly laughed at by the men. At this point Morgan fired a warning shot from his pistol. George gave the order to drop the cargo and retreat, but several of the younger men, led by Richard Wire, had brought long duck-guns with them. They stepped forward from their spot near the bathing machines and fired at Richard Morgan. Three shots struck him just below his left breast. A seaman called Michael Pickett was also wounded. Poor Morgan lingered for an hour or so and then expired. He was 34 years old and left a heartbroken widow.

Afterwards the coastal blockaders found thirty-three tubs of foreign rum. They were taken to the customs house at Dover.

George was more shaken than he cared to admit when Juliet next saw him. He fell through her door and just held her tightly for several minutes burying his nose in her hair while she held him. "I wish I could have stopped them from bringing the guns." He told Juliet; "They shouldn't have fired on that poor young officer!" He knew this would be the run that was to end the days of the Blues. "I won't be captured alive!" he told Juliet, much to her alarm and dread. "They sent two hundred officers to the village after the Battle of Brookland! By God, we managed to evade them then, so they won't take me alive this time!"

Six days later, at 1am on 6th August, some smugglers attacked some blockade men at Fort Moncrief, Hythe. They discharged their muskets at the men who formed a fighting party. They had discovered a party of smugglers - believed to be from Burmarsh - on the beach. They were unloading the cargo of a large galley. The fighting party encircled the men and fired on them. During this barrage three of the smugglers fell - one dead, one dying and one wounded. The others retreated, managing to take the large part of their cargo with them. Sadly for them, they left behind the badly wounded one of their party and fourteen tubs, were taken into the possession of the blockaders. The injured man was James Bushell from Hawkinge. He had been on runs with the Blues in the past. He had been shot through the knee. After initial treatment he subsequently required an amputation of the leg through the thigh. The blockade party would play the waiting game. Whilst he was unfit to give any information at that present time, they expected that, with the right care, he would make a very good recovery.

The gang lay low for a while. At 12 o'clock on the 2nd of August 1826 the funeral of Morgan had taken place in St Mary's church Dover. The coffin was preceded in military fashion by artilleryman and his hat (pierced by musket balls), pistols and cutlass were placed upon it. The pall bearers were six quartermasters and his weeping widow and comrades followed. He left no children. Morgan's Officer, Lieutenant Samuel Hellard, vowed to track down the persons responsible and to avenge his death.

An official poster was put around the county offering a reward of £500, more than a dozen year's salary for the average agricultural labourer, for information leading to arrests of the perpetrators. On the 2nd of September another gang member, Edward Horne from Ruckinge, was captured near Walmer Castle. At about 1.45am an armed party came down to the shore near Walmer Castle and called out to the sentinel there: "Don't fire mate, we won't hurt you!" At that moment a galley was observed near the beach. Two men ahead of the main party were carrying muskets under their arms. The sentinel drew his cutlass and challenged them, upon which they pointed their guns at him forcing him to parry them with his cutlass. These two men called out "Yo Ho" as a warning to the others and the main party then retreated towards Walmer village. The two armed men ran off towards the barracks. One of them got away, but the other dropped his musket. He was overtaken and arrested near the Standard boat house. He refused to give his name, but it proved to be Edward Horne.

The public had begun to think that the gang members had got away with murder. However, unbeknown to them, two of the gang were already in custody and they were prepared to turn Kings Evidence to save themselves. The net was closing in.

During this time Juliet worried herself half to death. She found her times with George even more precious but tinged with the sick fear that he would be taken and face the gallows. George made every effort to reassure her and tried to brave it out, but she could tell he was concerned. Every smuggler's dread was that one or more of their party would be captured and turn the rest of them in. Now it seemed likely that this would happen. A few of the gang took to sleeping away from their cottages. They lurked in barns and hayricks for fear of being captured in a raid. Aldington and surrounding villages had an air of apprehension and dread hanging over them.

George was more worried than he cared to admit. He needed to protect his family, particularly his eldest son, George, who managed his books and kept records for him. He wouldn't have his life put in jeopardy. Then there was Bet. He was sure she was with child again; how could she cope with a new baby, making ten children in all, on her own! These were worrying times that dampened any moments of happiness.

Taken in the night

Westron Wynde when wilt thou blow,
The smalle rayne downe can rayne
Cryst, yf my love were in my arms
And I yn my bed agayne!
Traditional

The autumn wore on and the nights drew in. The weather was blustery and damp. George called on Juliet and spent a passionate evening with her on the 17th of October. He left her at 9.30 in the evening, letting himself out of Laurel House as usual. Warm and sleepy from their lovemaking she stretched out in bed and fell asleep. She was awoken at 4.30 the next morning by a furious hammering on the door. Leaping from her bed and flinging a shawl round her shoulders,

Juliet flung wide the bedroom casement and leaned out into the thick, early morning frost.

John Ransley was below, with his horse in the moonlight of the early frosty morning – "Please Mrs Knatchbull, you must come quickly, they have taken George!"

Juliet's blood froze in her veins. A thousand thoughts rushed through her mind. John knew about them, who else knew? Where had they taken George? He would almost certainly hang! How did they find him? How could she live without her lover? But she told John that she would be down directly and called to wake Jane to let him in.

Grabbing her winter riding habit she struggled into it and pulled on her boots. She left her hair loose and threw her thick cloak around her shoulders. She must go to him wherever he was.

John was in the drawing room and Jane was lighting the fire when Juliet came down. He seemed calm but looked worried. Juliet got the impression of quiet strength and practicality from him.

When Hellard and his men had raided the Bourne Tap, Bet had sent her eldest son, George, to get John, who now told Juliet the following story, while they sipped piping hot tea brought in by Jane. Juliet then sent her to wake Josh and saddle her horse in readiness.

It seemed that Lieutenant Hellard had taken a party of sentries, and two Bow Street runners, from Fort Moncrief at Hythe and marched on to Aldington. They had silently surrounded the houses they wanted to make arrests in and taken the suspects. It was not known how they knew which houses to stake out. From there they had advanced to the Frith which they reached a little after 3am. They arrived at the Bourne Tap and cut the throats of the guard dogs so that they could not raise the alarm. Bursting through the door, they managed to catch George in his bedroom, still warm from sleep, struggling into his trousers.   He was handcuffed to the biggest strongest sentry in the party; then he and seven others from the village were marched off.

"They are taking them back to Fort Moncrief at Hythe," said John "but it is unlikely they will keep them there for long as they fear a rescue attempt from the locals."

According to the official report by Lieutenant Hellard - dated 18th October - the men seized were George Ransley, aged 44 years, Samuel and Robert Bailey, 36 and 30 years respectively. These were Bet's brothers. Charles Giles 28, Thomas Denard 21, Thomas Gilham (Dutchy) 24, and Richard 21 and William Wire 18 years were the other gang members taken. John asked Juliet if she could possibly get her cousin, Edward, to intervene. They needed to go to Ashford to Mr Platt, George's solicitor.

"I must find George first!", she cried, "I will ride and try to overtake them."

She promised John that she would petition her cousin and thanked him for letting her know. "Go and tell Mrs Ransley and the children that my cousin is informed and will be sure Mr Platt is engaged." She bade him, then she rushed to the stables yelling for Josh. Hurriedly mounting her horse, she galloped off towards the Hythe road hair and cloak streaming behind her as she rode.

She finally overtook them near Lympne. The men were marching, each man cuffed to a sentry and accompanied by the two Bow Street runners, Messrs Bishop and Smith. They were headed by Lieutenant Samuel Hellard.

George was astounded to see her and grinned with pleasure as she addressed Hellard from horseback, her hair streaming loose behind her, cloak flapping in the wind and her breath steaming in the thick early morning frost. "Lieutenant Hellard! I don't know which crime they are accused of, but these men are presumed innocent until proven guilty in a court of law. I therefore trust that they will be treated kindly and with dignity and respect. If any harm or misuse comes to any of them whilst in your care, my cousin, Sir Edward, shall hear of it, make no mistake!"

"Yes ma'am! Certainly ma'am!" Snapped the Lieutenant. George winked at her whilst some of the others sniggered.

"Mr Ransley!" She continued, "Rest assured, I'm away to my cousin and Mr Platt will be informed!" with that she wheeled her horse around and galloped off back towards Mersham.

For the first time since she had heard the news, tears blurred her vision on the dash back. She felt her throat become so tight that she thought she would choke. Her stomach was in a tight knot. They can't hang him! They mustn't hang him! But would any of them be able to prevent such a fate?

She reached Mersham Hatch by a quarter past seven. Her horse was taken to the stables for her and the maid showed her into the morning room. She lit the fire for her. Juliet sat huddled and pale, staring into the freshly lit fire until Fanny, Edward's wife, still in her dressing gown, greeted her. Seeing her red rimmed eyes she put her arms around her and held Juliet. she finally broke down sobbing.

Edward insisted that she joined them for breakfast. She ate but little; however, she drank some chocolate which restored her courage and strength. She related the whole tale of the arrests to Edward and Fanny. "They even slaughtered his dogs!" She cried; at which her tears began afresh. Edward instructed Fanny to care for her and send her home in his own carriage. His groom would return her horse later after it had been fed and rubbed down. He himself would ride straight to Ashford and notify Platt at once. With that Juliet had to be content.

"Edward knows, doesn't he?" Asked Juliet of Fanny. "About you and George?" Fanny asked, one eyebrow raised. Juliet blushed and lowered her eyes. "He doesn't judge you." Continued Fanny; "He knows how lonely one can be in widowhood. We just don't want you to be ill-used. Ransley can be a ruthless man, even if he does love you. He already has a wife and large family."

"I know that," replied Juliet, "but it's too late now, I love him and now he will hang!" "Not if Edward can help it!" retorted Fanny with conviction!

George and the others were immediately embarked on board the *Industry* for passage to HMS *Ramillies* at Deal. From there they would be transferred to the cutter *Antelope* which would take them to Deptford to be arraigned at Bow Street. They would be kept at Newgate to await trial. This was to be at Maidstone. To keep them in Kent beforehand was deemed too risky. Many a rescue by local people had been successful in previous cases.

Five years previously, the population had turned out in force in England's version of the storming of the Bastille! This occurred when a revenue officer called Billy 'Hellfire' Lilburn had caught eleven Folkestone and Sandgate smugglers on a run. He had them locked up in Dover gaol. Word soon got around, and the prisoners' fellows raised a huge mob which quickly broke down the gaol door. When it was discovered that the captured smugglers had been moved to the most secure cells, the mob started to, literally, pull the prison apart! They pelted with a hail of stones and tiles the troops that had, by then, been called in. The mayor of Dover arrived, but, when he attempted to read the riot act, he was set upon, and gave up. By this time, Lilburn himself had appeared. He tried (unsuccessfully) to persuade the commanding officer to fire on the crowd.

Eventually the smugglers were released, and made good their escape in hired horse-drawn carriages! They stopped at the *Red Cow* to have the conspicuous and unwieldy chains removed from their hands; meanwhile outside the mob continued to rampage through the town, smashing windows.

The gaol was damaged beyond repair and a new one had to be constructed.

Custody and Court

'Those vain delusions to maintain,
We practised every art to gain,
We took a sinful course abroad,
And many people did defraud.'
Ransley brothers execution song

Edward and George seemed to have some history. Certainly they were civil to each other when they met, and Juliet knew that her cousin was an habitual recipient of George's smuggled goods. They were not in the same social circle, and yet there was a quiet familiarity between them which Juliet couldn't quite fathom.

Edward himself had family problems. His younger brother John Knatchbull, whilst enjoying the same privileges and education as Edward, had wasted it. He had started out well and had become a captain in the Royal Navy, but somehow he had missed his first ship and had to be reappointed another. After the battle of Waterloo, where Juliet's beloved husband, James, had been killed, he was retired from the Navy on full pay, but had incurred huge debts in the Azores.

The Admiralty stopped his pay because of this. Two years previously, in the August of 1824, he had been found guilty of robbery with force whilst carrying arms, and was transported for 14 years to New South Wales on the *Asia*. Edward had felt the family shame. However, none of the local people seemed aware of John's criminal history or of his fate. Juliet wondered if George had found out and had helped them somehow, or had come to some sort of financial understanding with Edward.

Certainly the Hatch was huge and had numerous outbuildings and vast grounds. These could be good hiding places for contraband goods, she mused. She knew that every trip to the continent to buy the uncustomed goods, had to be financed by an 'Investor'. Could Edward have been an investor at one time she wondered? There must have been something between the two of them, thought Julia to herself. As a local Magistrate, Edward had fined George £100, on at least two occasions. George told her that the fines were never paid.

Once goods were seized from the Bourne Tap and taken to Ashford for auction. Later that night, apparently, they were all quietly returned.

Edward certainly did not need any adverse family history, nor any whiff of scandal broadcast. He was also rising through the ranks, both politically and in his law practice. He had a bright future ahead of him.

Mr Platt was engaged and rushed to London directly. On Friday the 27th of October 1826 George and the seven other gang members were arraigned at Bow Street Magistrates Court. Londoners flocked to the area to catch a glimpse of real life smugglers! George and his accomplices enjoyed the same heroic adoration of the people as Robin Hood had all those centuries beforehand. At around half past twelve they were brought to the office and charged with the wilful murder of Richard Morgan, First Class Quartermaster of H.M.S. *Ramillies,* on the beach at Dover.

Great excitement, particularly amongst the female element, ran through the public gallery as the prisoners were led in. They were all defiantly dressed in their blue smocks (the traditional uniform of the smuggling gang and from which their epithet, the Blues, was derived. The exception was George. He was described as a fine looking man, very handsome in his shooting jacket, made of fustian.

Juliet herself couldn't bear to be present but John was there and had promised to report back faithfully to her on the entire proceedings.

Sir Richard Birnie was the Bow Street Magistrate examining the prisoners and Mr Jones, solicitor to the Admiralty, was prosecuting. The very able Mr Platt was for the defence. They were then formally charged with the wilful murder of Richard Morgan on the 30th of July, and also with unlawfully assembling in arms, with the intention of running smuggled goods, on the Kentish coast.

Mr Jones for the Prosecution brought forward a material witness. To the Consternation of George and the gang, in came Edward Horne who had been captured near Walmer on the 2nd September. To save himself, he had turned Kings Evidence. He was called to bear witness against the gang. He maintained that George had not been armed. He never knew him to carry arms, he stated emphatically. The prosecution also had James Bushell, somewhat recovered now. He was waiting, reluctantly, to give evidence against the gang.

Mr Platt fought valiantly. Sir Richard Birnie said that he knew George Ransley had met him before by appointment; at which Mr Platt interjected that, unless Mr Jones intended to bring forward

54

charges other than murder against his client, it was not necessary to state the business on which these appointments took place. Mr Jones stated that he had at least thirty distinct charges against the prisoner, but Mr Platt cut him short. "It is not exactly fair, nor is it customary with the Crown, to excite prejudice against a prisoner in this manner." He exclaimed.

Sir Richard Birnie, said that he was sorry that his question had been the cause of exciting these observations. And so it went on, with Mr Platt parrying every point with his skill and legal knowledge.

The outcome, however, was that the prisoners were fully committed to Newgate prison to await trial. This would be held in Maidstone. Mr Jones had stated that: "they needed to be confined in a place more secure than the Kentish coast, as it was a notorious fact that smugglers had broken open, or pulled down, every prison in that part of the county and five years previously they had broken open the gaol at Dover in broad daylight and rescued fifteen of their gang!"

All are gathered in

'Cage an Eagle and it will bite at the wires,
Be they of Iron or Gold.'
Henrik Ibsen – The Vikings of Helgeland

John Ransley brought news of the proceedings to Juliet on his return from London. Jane had let him in and they sat either side of the fire in the drawing room sipping fine Madeira wine. By the firelight, when glimpsed at a certain angle, John could have been George sitting there. It tugged at her heartstrings and she felt a tightening in her throat. True, he was almost 10 years younger - nearer her own age. His hair was thicker, he was a few inches taller and his top teeth straighter, but he was very much like her George. Not that George could ever have really been her George, even if he had remained a free man. He had his family, his wife; but, Oh! How could she live without him?

In the November, on a wild and stormy night of torrential rain, several more of George's associates had been taken. They were Paul Pierce, Edward Pantry, James Quested (the brother of the hanged Cephas), Richard Higgins, Thomas Wheeler, the Folkestone blacksmith, James Hogben, John Bailey - one of Bet's uncles - James Wilson, James Smeed and John Horne.

Edward Pantry turned Kings Evidence as soon as he could and betrayed his fellow gang members! John Horne did the same a little later on. Paul Pearce had been not been found during the October arrests. He was living in a very old house in Bonnington village which had a wide chimney. He had hidden up this chimney until the danger had passed, by which time he was almost suffocated with heat and dust!

It is said that their loved ones were not given a chance to say goodbye. They were not informed as to where their folk were to be taken. Knowing that their crimes carried a death sentence should they be found guilty, they must have been incandescent with worry. These were troubling times for everybody concerned.

All of them were arraigned on the 23rd November before Sir Richard Birnie, and charged with the same offences as the others. They joined them in Newgate. The trial was set for the 6th January

1827 at Maidstone. Mr Platt told Edward that their only hope was to try a plea bargain and, thereby, rely on the mercy of the Solicitor General.

Juliet felt that her life had been suspended. She was numb with misery. Samuel, her son, came home for Christmas and she hugged him to her, taking some comfort from the boy's presence. She threw all her energies into his wellbeing, but she was quite distracted and withdrawn. They were both invited to The Hatch for Christmas day. Juliet took some comfort from the festivities there and seeing the excitement on Samuel's face, but Fanny and Edward were worried about her. She was quiet, withdrawn and pale.

On the feast of St Stephen, the day after Christmas day, Edward was riding with the hunt and Fanny, Juliet, Samuel and Edward's children all went to see them off and take a stirrup cup with them. "Good morning Mrs Knatchbull!" She heard a familiar rich voice. Turning, she saw John Ransley mounted on his high-bred horse, horn cup in hand. How handsome he looked in his red jacket, highly polished jockey boots and tight cravat, she thought. "Good morning to you, Sir! I hope you have a pleasant one!" She replied. She felt herself blush. Edward and Fanny watched her. As Edward and John rode off with the hunt Fanny drew her aside.

"I know John has been bringing you news from London." She told Juliet. "John Ransley is a really fine fellow. His side of the family were always more well-to-do, even if some of them have lost their way in the past. Edward says what a good tenant he is and how successful he is with his wool business." Juliet merely smiled. "He has kept me informed of developments with George and his associates." That was all she would say. Arm in arm they walked back to the house, watching the children playing ahead of them.

John started to call upon Juliet on a regular basis seemingly to check that she was coping without George. He told her that the trial date was set and asked if she wound be going to it. Bet, heavy with child, would be attending for part of the trial, he told her. It was expected that the town would be crowded to capacity for this trial. It was the talk of the county. Juliet thought it might be advisable to attend with Edward accompanying her. She felt sure that she could persuade Edward. Hard as it would be, it could be the last time she ever saw George in this world.

Mr Platt and Mr Clarkson were appearing for the defence. "Can Platt get them off the murder charge?" Juliet asked John. "He is working on just that issue. It is said that he might be able to come to an arrangement with regard to the plea. If they admit to the other charges, they may yet be spared the murder charge. After all, it may prove a difficulty to establish whom it was who fired the fatal shot, so that lies in their favour." John went on: "In either case, the best we could hope for would be transportation."

Juliet felt her stomach knot and a wave of nausea pass over her. She would never again feel his arms around her, look up at his handsome face above her, or hear his voice whispering in her ear. She would never again kiss that neck - that same neck might well have a noose around it very soon! She could not bear to think about it. Transportation would be better than death, for at least then he would be under the same sky as her, under the same stars. Perhaps she might hear news of him through John.

She made up her mind to take action. "My cousin is a friend of the Attorney General." She told John, "I shall petition him and ask him to intervene. We will save them if we can!"

Lovers by a gate – F Scalini

A Final Farewell

'If there ever comes a day when we can't be together
Keep me in your heart. I'll stay there forever'
A.A. Milne Winnie the Pooh

George had written a note to Juliet which he had entrusted to John to deliver to her. In it he thanked her for enriching his life during the past few months and he bade her be brave. He said he loved her very much and, whatever the outcome of his trial, that would not change. He had cherished the times they had spent together. She would always be special to him and he would love her and keep her in his heart for as long as he had breath in his body. He also loved his wife and so Juliet must try to forget him. She must continue on with her life since he would no longer be there for her.

Wherever he was destined to go he would always think of her fondly and keep a special place for her in his heart. He hoped that she could forgive him for not being there and find eventual happiness. He finished the note with a declaration of his love for her and placed several kisses at its ending.

Juliet found it difficult to read through her unshed tears, and she had a large lump in her throat. She would always cherish it.

Juliet visited Mersham. After dinner, she caught Edward alone in his study. "You are friends with the Sir Charles, the Attorney General, are you not, Edward?" she began. She explained to him how hard it would be on the village folk if the Blues were executed. "Fifty children will be orphaned! Imagine the strain upon the parish that that will cause! The Union will be bursting at the seams. How would that look in your constituency?" And she cajoled him further: "I wonder what your colleagues in the House of Commons would say if they knew how your drinks cellar was stocked or where Fanny's lace petticoats came from?"

Edward gave a wry smile. "Blackmail little becomes you, cousin! Do not worry for we are both on the same side here. Tory I may be but my views towards our villagers are liberal. I will speak as you wish. I know Sir Charles both from my college days at Oxford and latterly from Lincolns Inn also. I often see him at the House of Commons. Leave it in my hands. I shall speak with him and see if we cannot save your Ransley's neck!" And with that, he took her arm and led her through to join Fanny.

****

Two days before the trial began Edward paid a visit to Lincolns Inn in London. He was going from there to Maidstone for the trial, and Juliet would be joining him there on the night before. She had finally managed to convince him to let her attend. He was not very pleased with the idea, but she had stood firm and proclaimed that she would attend with or without his escort! She prevailed. On his London trip, Edward insisted on buying dinner for his old friend, Sir Charles Wetherell, the Attorney General. After a very good meal they sat chatting over port wine.

"The trial of these smugglers from my constituency,,," began Edward. He told Sir Charles of how the villages would suffer ruination if the menfolk were hung. He explained how fifty children would be orphaned. He expounded on how all the widows would be dependent on the parish. He concluded by saying that Ransley had seemingly endless resources, and was prepared to fight all of the way. The trial could run on for months, costing the country dearly. He also hinted that some high-born names could be dragged through the mire. Finally he came to the point: "By the way how is your little dalliance with the flame-haired actress going? I do hope your wife hasn't found out yet!"

Sir Charles smiled slowly. "I think we understand each other." He said sagely. He nodded. "Get Platt to pay me a visit. I am sure we can come to some conclusion over their plea. I will instruct my subordinate, the Solicitor General, to intervene!"

****

George, in his cell at Maidstone gaol, had plenty of time to think. He knew that they were all facing the death sentence. However, he also knew that Platt was good - very good - and he, George, was financing the defence of them all. He took stock. He had resources to give them a long run for their money and the gang had already cost his Majesty's government a pretty penny in lost revenue. True, they had Bushell and Horne and they would save themselves by turning Kings Evidence; he knew that. They were not made of the same stuff as Cephas Quested. But who could blame them? Bushell, in particular, had suffered, and due to his amputation, through the thigh - high near the hip - he would find future work difficult. Doubtless he also wanted a share of the reward money. Hopefully Platt could come up with some sort of deal. He knew too, that Juliet and her Cousin, Edward Knatchbull, were working behind the scenes for them. It would be well, it had to be well! Juliet. She brought a smile to his lips. What a woman! He missed the softness of her skin, the way she smelt - expensive and upper class. He missed the feel of her hair. He longed to love her just one more time. In different circumstances of birth, they might have made a formidable couple. Now, she must live on without him. He had Bet to consider. Bet and their children - and the new one, due any day now! If he were spared and received a second chance, Bet and the family would be his main consideration. Cousin John would take care of Juliet, George knew that; John admired her greatly. He was a good man and would be better for her.

However, little did any of the Blues, or their associates, know that the Crown Prosecution had one more major trick up their collective sleeves.

Two local men, desirous of the reward money had decided to throw George and the others to the wolves. William Marsh was a farmer's son and a one-time look out for the Blues. James Spratford had, at one time, been one of the smugglers himself. He was an ex signaller for the Royal Navy and used this knowledge to inform the coastal blockade of the gang's movements. In 1800 he had been the parish overseer and had known many of the gang since their childhood. Spratford had been a traitor in the midst of the Blues for some time. It was he who had shown Lieutenant Hellard where most of the men lived on the nights they were arrested. He knew them all well, and had done so for many years. This would certainly make his betrayal of his former friends and allies even harder to understand let alone forgive.

Trial at Maidstone

'My Geordie shall hang in chains of gold
Such chains, as never were many
Because he comes from noble birth
And is loved by a virtuous lady!'
Traditional ballad

The Trial opened on the 6th of January 1827. The town of Maidstone was packed with people, all in a state of great excitement. They were eager to catch a glimpse of the latter-day Robin Hoods, the infamous Aldington Gang. Accommodation was at a premium and many of the subpoenaed witnesses and prisoners wives had to share rooms (and sometimes beds). Many of the wives had travelled up, including a very heavily pregnant Bet Ransley.

Luckily for Juliet, Edward had secured comfortable lodgings for them within a friend's hunting lodge at Loose. This was but a short drive away and had been opened up especially for them.

Juliet could eat no breakfast. She felt sick with anxiety for George. As they arrived at the Courthouse a little before nine o'clock in the morning, the doors were being besieged by a huge sea of people, all eager to attend the trial of the infamous gang. Mr Justice Park took his seat on the bench at nine o'clock precisely and the court was filled instantly!

The following prisoners were put to the bar first: Robert Bailey, Samuel Bailey, Thomas Denard, Thomas Gilham, James Hogben, George Ransley, James Smeed, Thomas Wheeler, Richard Wire and William Wire.

Juliet had overheard some of the witnesses talking outside. They were saying how foolish it had been arresting little William Wire since he never carried a firearm and was only a 'look out' for the gang. It was widely believed that Richard Wire, the bigger, elder, brother had been the one to pull the trigger when Morgan was shot. However, all agreed that William would have wanted to be with his brother wherever that might be, in either life or death. He was his hero and the brothers meant the world to each other. John Horne and Edward Pantry had turned Kings Evidence and so would not be charged. (It did them no good in the end, for, shortly after the trial, they were both caught sheep stealing and transported!)

Juliet held her breath as George was led in. All the prisoners had leg irons on which were chained. They all looked well and cared for except James Wilson, who seemed pale and had visibly lost weight. George looked hale and hearty and quite handsome as he walked in, as jauntily as the irons would allow. He scanned the courtroom and smiled at his wife, then, facing away from his wife he saw Juliet. He winked at her before being urged forward by the guards. Juliet looked at the ground to control her emotions.

Bet had travelled with Charles Giles' wife, Mary, and Richard Higgins' wife, Rhoda, who was also her sister. They were all staying in a public house in Maidstone.

The indictment charged the prisoners with "assembling with other persons unknown, to the number thirty, armed with firearms, at the parish of St James the Apostle, of the Port of Dover, in the county of Kent, on the 30th July; and that Richard Wire did then and there unlawfully, maliciously and feloniously shoot Richard Morgan three mortal wounds under the left pap of his breast, of which wounds he languished, and languishingly did live for the space of one hour, and then did die".

The other prisoners were charged with being present, aiding, assisting and comporting the said Richard Wire in the commission of the said murder. The prisoners all pleaded 'not guilty.'

The Solicitor General, Sir Nicholas Conyngham- Tindal, Mr Horace Twiss and Mr Knox were Counsel for the Crown; Mr Platt and Mr Clarkson were for the prisoners.

At this point a consultation of some length was held between Counsels of both sides which ended with a communication to Mr Justice Park.

His Lordship then ordered all the other untried prisoners to be brought from the gaol and then the following were put to the bar: John Bailey, Richard Higgins, Paul Pierce, James Wilson (who still seemed very pale and was coughing throughout), Samuel Bailey, Thomas Denard, Thomas Gilham, James Smeed and George Ransley.

They were indicted for "assembling, with numerous others unknown, on the 16th of March at New Romney, armed with firearms, to aid and assist in the landing and running uncustomed goods".

There were various other counts against them, one of which charged them with feloniously, wilfully and maliciously shooting at Patrick Doyle and Cluryn McCarthy, persons employed by His Majesty's customs for the prevention of smuggling.

John Bailey was arraigned first. He pleaded guilty. The learned judge said that he "was aware that they were in the hands of able and learned gentlemen of the bar, so he had no doubt they were acting under the advice of their counsel. He should explain to them the consequence of pleading guilty, but as they were assisted by their learned counsel, he would refrain from interposing his personal opinion!"

Various local witnesses had been subpoenaed to appear but William Marsh and James Spratford came forward voluntarily, out of greed, to claim the reward money. George looked crushed and somewhat hurt when he saw them. Juliet was furious with them as she had overheard James Spratford saying outside the court that "Ransley and Dick Wire are bound to hang. If they do, I shall stay and see them swing." The other local witnesses expressed their hope that this would not be the outcome and they would certainly not wish to witness such a melancholy spectacle! Most of them had known George and the others since they were small, all playmates together, and most of them did not want to be there.

Juliet's attention was brought back to the proceedings. All the other prisoners pleaded guilty to their several indictments. The ten prisoners charged with the murder were then left at the bar and the jury were enrolled.

The Solicitor General stood to speak. Juliet strained her ears and held her breath. Her palms were hurting where she was digging her fingernails into them so hard. She bit her lower lip with anxiety.

The Solicitor General then stated that "the prisoners having pleaded guilty to the other charges, by which they had forfeited their lives to the laws of their country, (at this Juliet felt her insides churn and her mouth went dry - she visibly paled) it was not his intention to offer any evidence against them on the charge of murder. He could not say that their lives would be saved - Juliet felt sick at hearing this - as far as his recommendation would go, they should have the benefit of it, but at all events they would most probably be sent out of the country for the remainder of their lives."

Juliet looked gratefully at Edward on hearing this, He stared stonily ahead. By this arrangement Robert Bailey, who lived at Mersham and Thomas Wheeler, the blacksmith from Folkestone were wholly acquitted as they had only been indicted for the murder. They left the court and returned home on the same day.

The remaining fourteen prisoners, who had pleaded guilty, were then put to the bar: John Bailey and Paul Pierce, from Bonnington, Samuel Bailey, Charles Giles and Richard Higgins, from Bilsington, James Hogben, from Ruckinge , George Ransley, Thomas Denard and Thomas Gilham from Aldington Frith, James Quested from Hawkinge, James Smeed, James Wilson and Richard and William Wire all from Aldington.

Mr Justice Park then addressed the prisoners. He told them that they had pleaded guilty to an offence of a most heinous nature. They had assembled in numerous bodies to aid in the running of uncustomed goods and in so doing had fired upon persons who were only doing their duty. At this point Juliet's mind wandered off to how she would cope without him. She watched him and her mind wandered back to the happy and passionate times they had spent together.

She was brought back to the proceedings by Mr Justice Park saying that, due to the darkness of the night, it may be difficult to fix upon all of them the crime of murder. Perhaps no human eye saw the hand that committed the said murder, but they had all pleaded guilty to a very serious offence.

In his opinion His Lordship, the Solicitor General, had exercised a sound discretion, but had dealt with the prisoners most humanely; for if any of them had been convicted of the murder they would certainly have been executed on the Monday next. His Lordship disclaimed being in any way a party to the lenient course that had been adopted, for he should not feel warranted in recommending them to the mercy of the sovereign, although the Solicitor General had promised to do so and would doubtless keep his word. The prisoners had admitted to forming gangs of up to eighty persons - numerous to overcome the peaceable part of the community. These things could not go on with impunity. It must be made known throughout the country that, if an offence of this nature were again committed, no mercy would be shown to the offenders.

His Lordship then stated: "If persons in the highest stations in life were not to purchase smuggled goods, there would soon be an end to smuggling; but many laboured under the delusion that defrauding the revenue was no crime." At this point Edward went quite red and ran his fingers around the inside of his stock at the neck to loosen it). He continued: "He trusted that if the mercy of our gracious sovereign were extended to the prisoners, he trusted they would receive it with due gratitude and be still more grateful to their God, whom they had so grievously offended.

He then passed the sentence of death on the prisoners in the usual form. The calendar states that: 'the smugglers are to be executed on the 5th of February, but it is not expected any of them will suffer.'

The prisoners were then removed from court.

****

Bet and the other wives wailed as the sentence was passed. A collective gasp ran around the courtroom. George and the other prisoners looked stonily ahead as they were sentenced, but George smiled up at her as he left the room. It was the last time Juliet would ever set eyes on him.

She sat with her eyes closed for a few minutes. She could not trust her legs to hold her should she try to stand and the lump in her throat threatened to choke her. Eventually she felt Edward gently holding her elbow to guide her out and she looked pleadingly at him.

"All will be well." He assured her. "I will speak to Platt. I am sure the Solicitor General will keep his word."

Life without Love

'I am one who loved not wisely, but too well
William Shakespeare, Othello act 5 scene 2'

The prisoners had left court under sentence of death! Juliet could neither sleep nor eat. She walked around feeling numb, with knotted stomach and a lump in her throat. The execution was scheduled for the 5th of February. On Saturday the 3rd, John called in to see her. "Mr Platt has just told me that Mr Agar, the Governor of the County Goal in Maidstone, received a letter Thursday last. It was from the Secretary of State saying that the death sentence on George and the rest of them has been respited. They are to be taken on Monday next, the 5th, for the purpose of transportation for life to Van Dieman's Land. George, James Wilson, Charles Giles, James Hogben, James

Quested and the Wire bothers are to be taken to Portsmouth to the *Leviathan*. John and Sam Bailey, Thomas Denard, Thomas Gilham, Dick Higgins, Paul Pierce and James Smeed are going to the *York* at Gosport."

Transportation for life! Juliet felt immense relief that his life would be spared, but how could she live without him? The room swayed as John told her this news and her ears were buzzing. She visibly paled and sat down hard on the chair behind her. John called for Jane to bring brandy to her mistress and started chaffing Juliet's hands. She rallied herself and thanked him. Gratefully sipping the brandy, she asked after Bet and the children and the other families. "Bet and the children will be joining him out there once the baby is born and strong enough to travel; also she has to settle her affairs here." John told her. "The others all want to go out too. Betsy and the Baileys will have no problem affording it, but some of the others will have to rely on the generosity of the parish." Juliet knew straight away that her mission for the next few months would be to push for the parish funds to send the poorer families out to Van Diemen's Land to be reunited with their loved ones. That is if they survived the prison hulks first; and the gruelling journey out there.

The next few weeks were like a dream to Juliet. She ate without tasting, slept without resting, and her dreams were fitful. She felt as though she were in a perpetual trance-like state. On the 18th of

February, just a couple of weeks after George had been taken to the prison hulk, Bet gave birth to a daughter. She named her Elizabeth after herself. She was a puny, sickly child and suffered frequent abdominal complaints. Bet blamed it on the stress she had suffered during the last few weeks of her pregnancy.

The child frequently suffered from swelling of her abdomen and purging requiring several visits to the village dispensary. Aldington was not a happy place to be at this time. Fifty children were rendered fatherless by the transportation of the Blues. There was much financial hardship.

Edward Horne and James Bushell had been forced to turn Kings Evidence due to their capture by the blockade forces. That way they were exempted from charges and Bushell could receive the care he needed to survive his injuries. They were each awarded £100 of the £500 reward money since their testimonies had been of the most use. William Marsh and James Spratford received £130 each - they had come forward voluntarily, out of greed and spite!

Lieutenant C.A. Johnson, who had captured Horne, and James Ash who had captured Bushell, were each awarded £20.

Marsh took his share of the reward money and left the area. This was a wise move on his behalf. Spratford returned to Aldington and decided to brazen it out! It behoved him not at all. The local women burned him in effigy outside his own house. None of the local tradesmen would serve him, which forced him to travel further and further afield for his needs. The local barber refused to shave him - he stated that the temptation to slit his throat would be too great. The reward money did little good for him, as time would tell.

The York Hulk

Transportation

'Crying Oh! Oh! my love is gone
He's the one I adore, He's gone,
And I never shall see him no more!'
The Constant Lovers. Traditional song

George and the others were sent off to the hulks. It was said that you could smell the boats before ever you saw them in the distance. The disgusting smell of stagnant bilge water, rancid food and humanity packed too closely together in foul conditions told its own sorry tale. Only the strong and robust could survive them. They were, in fact, derelict men-of–war ships, divested of all fittings, masts, sails, wheels and anything that could possibly enable them to be sailed. They were then moored in groups as floating prisons, off Portsmouth, Deptford, Gosport, Sheerness and Woolwich.

There were usually libraries on board and the better educated were encouraged to use them. However, there was little free time. If you were a cook, you had to rise at 3am to prepare the disgusting coarse barley boiled in water to make a sort of porridge which tasted of nothing. An average daily timetable was -

5.30 am all hands were woken.

5.45 muster on deck for breakfast then swab decks.

6.45am Stow hammocks then proceed to shore for a day's labour.

12 noon Dinner.

1.20pm Labour recommences.

5.45pm Return to the hulk check irons, searched for improper concealment.

6.30pm School.

7.30pm Chapel, muster, lock up

9.00pm Lights out and lock down

Saturday evenings, every prisoner had to wash and shave ready for divine service on Sunday.

Their life on board these hell holes is best describes by James Tucker (1808 – 1888) who writes in 'Ralph Rashleigh, Life on the Leviathan Hulk'. This was written circa 1840 but not published until 1952:

Lags away" was the cry that warned those who were transported that the time had now arrived for their removal to the hulk; and shortly afterwards those who had been given respite from death were placed in two large vans, strongly ironed, handcuffed and chained together, as well as to the van, which drove off at a rapid rate to an unknown destination. By driving continuously, only stopping to change horses, the van made the Portsmouth dockyard the following afternoon and they were permitted to alight on a wooden wharf, outside of which lay the gloomy bulk of the old Leviathan.

This vessel, an ancient 74, after having for many years borne the victorious banner of Britain over the navigable world, was at last condemned to the vile purpose of a convict hulk, stripped of all that makes for a ship's vanity. Just two masts remained to serve as clothes props. The newly arrived criminals were paraded upon the quarterdeck of this old, desecrated hooker, mustered, and received by the captain of the hulk, after which the irons they had brought with them were taken off and given back to the gaol authorities, who now departed. The convicts in the meantime were all marched to the forecastle and ushered into a washing-room, where each man was obliged to strip, get into a large tub of water, and cleanse himself thoroughly. Each then received a suit of coarse grey clothing consisting of a jacket, waistcoat and trousers. A very rough twilled cotton shirt, striped with blue and white, a round-crowned broad-brimmed felt hat, and a pair of heavily-nailed shoes completed this unique costume; and when they had been divested of their whiskers and got their hair closely cropped, the metamorphosis was complete. Here, too, each man was double-

ironed with a pair of heavy fetters, and after this they again emerged on deck, where a hammock and two blankets, with a straw palliasse, were to supplied every new prisoner, and they were now ordered to go below.

They followed one of the guards down what seemed an endless succession of step-ladders. When they reached the bottom, a perfect chaos of sounds saluted their ears. The first glimpse of the lower deck of this convict hulk showed a long passage bordered by iron palisading, with lamps hung at regular intervals. Within these rows of palisades were wooden partitions, which subdivided the deck into upwards of a score of apartments. In each of these about fifteen or twenty convicts slept and ate.

The author goes on to tell how the cry of: "New Chums, new chums" went up amid howls of jeering laughter when the new convicts were brought down. Then the old chums played pranks on the new so that they 'slept but little' on their first night, waking to the stench of a wooden tub containing breakfast, a 'food composed of a very coarse kind of barley boiled up with the soup made from the meat which was allowed to the convicts every alternate day. The diet of the hulk, exclusive of meat and barley soup, was, three days in each week, a portion of a mysterious semi-petrification, very much akin to chalk both in taste and durability. Nay, it was even much harder; but by the courtesy of the contractors dubbed for the nonce cheese - 'too big to *swallow and too hard to bite'. For breakfast and supper, when meat was not allowed, each man received a pint of the barley before named, plain boiled in water. Besides the above articles, a pound of very black unpalatable bread formed the daily allowance of each man, with a pint of very bad vinegar, here dignified with the name of table beer.*

******

In March, news came to Aldington that James Wilson had succumbed to his illness and had died of consumption on the 15th of February aboard the *Leviathan.* He was 29 years old and left a mother alone in Aldington. There was much sorrow and many prayers for him and his poor mother in the village. What happened to him then is best described by James Tucker again:

One day three patients died, and as deceased convicts were then usually buried in a graveyard near a number of ruined buildings on the Gosport side called 'Rat's Castle', some of the convalescent patients were selected to go there and dig the graves. Accordingly, over the water they went, under the care of one of the old sailors in a boat manned by the convicts.

The soil was very light, and their task an easy one. When it was done the guard made a signal by waving a handkerchief upon a stick. While they were awaiting the return of their boat they lay or sat among the nameless, shapeless grassy mounds which filled the convicts' graveyard, each marking the narrow resting-place of one who had died degraded, forgotten and unknown, his last moments uncheered by the voice of affection or the soothing sympathies of kindred, and whose remains were scarcely cold ere he was hurried into the rude shell, hustled off in the boat, amid jokes or oaths, as the prevailing mood of the boatmen might be, and finally thrust in the ground, without a prayer, scarcely six inches below the surface of the earth.

It was with huge relief and grateful prayers that Juliet heard that they had been transferred to the *Governor Ready* on the 3rd of April, for transfer to Hobart. Her relief was only exceeded by that of George and the others, who must have been in a miserable and wretched condition waiting to board her from both the *York* and the *Leviathan.* The Ship was built on Prince Edward Island and was a typical convict transport ship of 500 tons. She sailed from Portsmouth on that 3rd of April 1827 carrying 192 male convicts. One man (not one of our Kentish men) was to die on the three month voyage. Conditions were very much better on these ships than they were on the hulks.

First each man had to strip and be thoroughly cleansed and examined to make sure they were medically fit to travel. Then they were issued with a new set of clothes. Rations were a great improvement on the slop served on the hulks. They were better than those issued to the men of the Royal Navy. Their education was catered for with libraries and lessons. They were encouraged to sing and dance and sometimes they were allowed to help to sail the ship. Sleeping conditions were better too. Each man had 18 inches of sleeping space compared to the Royal Navy who had to make do with just 14 inches for each man.

They arrived in Hobart on the 31st day of July 1827 and by August the 12th they were assigned. George's farming experience stood him in very good stead since he was assigned to a free-settler farmer and had almost unlimited freedom as there was nowhere he could escape to. The others with skills or trades were similarly placed. The word was put out to the populace of Hobart that the latest consignment of convicts from England were a useful bunch of men, especially the ones from Kent, as they had a mass of farming experience between them.

Most were put to farming or horticulture, Charles Giles was initially put into the police force as was James Smeed. Giles was eventually to return to his old trade of shoemaker.

Juliet gained great comfort from her son, Samuel, at this time. When he was away at school she wrote regularly and sent him many parcels. Edward and Fanny were concerned for her and tried to cheer her with dinner parties and outings to friends' houses, but she was in a very sad place and could not be comforted. Since the day George had been captured in his bedroom, Juliet had not shed any more tears. She felt constantly empty, lost and aching.

John was her comfort and support at this time as he called upon her regularly and brought her news, as he heard it, of George and the others. She busied herself with supporting the families of the transported men and going on long drives with her horse and gig. She felt in a constant trance-like state and in much emotional pain.

In late April, after she heard about the transfer to the convict ship, Juliet was driving past farmland in Mersham on her way home from the Hatch. She glanced at a man in the field as she passed by and saw that it was John. He was herding sheep and lambs. On impulse she stopped her gig and alighted. Tethering the horse to a tree, she climbed the stile into the field calling to John as she went. He had just picked up a tiny lamb, just a few hours old, which had managed to escape to the wrong side of the fold and away from its distraught mother.

He smiled tenderly at her and placed the lamb in Juliet's arms to hold for a moment. She cradled it to her breast and felt its warmth, its softness and its vulnerability. It had the tip of its little pink tongue sticking out of its mouth and its eyes were closed.

Juliet felt a sudden sorrow, for this little vulnerable, beautiful and fragile creature, to be born into this cruel and heartless world. Her eyes filled with tears and she shook with great silent sobs. Hot tears coursed down her face and splashed onto the warm woolly coat of the lamb. Finally all her pent up emotions had risen to the surface, she handed the lamb to John, who placed it under its mother. As she covered her face with her hands and her body was wracked with sobs, she felt that she would never be able to stop. John wrapped his arms around her and pulled her to him. She clung to him as he held her tight for a time until her tears subsided. Then she turned her tear-stained face up towards him. The kiss, when it came, was no surprise to either of them. Juliet had finally realised how much she needed and wanted him. She had fallen in love with a Ransley again! This time it was guilt free, their love was untarnished by any forbidden law. They were both free to give their hearts and bodies to each other without fear of causing damage to anyone else. Finally they had found true happiness in each other. John had always admired Juliet for her intelligence and wit, but, best of all, he admired her looks. Juliet found him charming, intelligent and well mannered. In his mid-thirties, he had a pleasant face, brown hair and blue eyes. He was of average height. She thought him rather attractive, with a great knowledge of farming.....

After The Blues

'The evil that men do lives after them;
The good is oft interred with their bones'
William Shakespeare- Julius Caesar act 3 Scene 2

So we leave John and Juliet, lost each other's charms. But what of the real people left behind in this drama? What really happened in court to get the men's sentence commuted to transportation for life? There could have been a number of reasons. Undoubtedly George Ransley had plenty of resources to keep the case going on and on. The trial would have been fought long and hard thus incurring great expense for the prosecution. It is more than probable that he could have dragged a few important people in high positions though the mire. Mr. Justice Park intimated that people in elevated positions were involved in receiving smuggled goods, so that would have embarrassed more than a few.

Mr. Platt was wily and resourceful. He would have dragged out each point of conflicting evidence and contested them - the way he had contested the visibility on the day Morgan was shot. He also intimated to the Solicitor General, in their lengthy consultation in court, that all of the prisoners were ready to plead guilty to the lesser charges, provided that their lives would be spared, understanding that they would be transported overseas for the remainder of their lives. This would be a happy arrangement for the people from the higher echelons, for if the gang were out of the country, their secrets would be safe and they could not be implicated in any way. If, on the other hand they knew they were to die, they had nothing to lose by revealing all that they knew.

The other reason was most probably political. The country was on the brink of revolution. Not very many years had passed since the 'Rights of Man' bill had been passed in France. Although the protests in England were largely bloodless, at that moment in time, it could have been otherwise. Just a few short years later the Swing riots would be happening and workers would be fighting for 2 shillings and sixpence per day (fifteen shillings a week) in summer.

Enclosure was happening and acres of common and valuable grazing land, was being taken away from the poorer people. Indeed Aldington Frith, near the Bourne Tap, had all been open common with donkeys and sheep grazing. After the Blues were transported Mr.

Deedes, the Lord of the Manor of Sandling Park, Hythe, took it and enclosed it. He, being a kindly man, did, at least, give all the commoners a little plot of the land first.

With riot and revolution around the corner, how would it have looked to the ordinary working man if fourteen simple villagers were hung in a mass 'turning off' on Penenden Heath? And this for trying to improve the lot of the common man by avoiding customs on a few goods! Not the best public relations exercise for the Government, you might say.

George Ransley brought prosperity to the area. He paid the average scout and tub carrier eight shillings per night and twenty shillings to his batsmen. Free ale, biscuit (big biscuits at a penny a piece) and cheese were thrown in, all funded by George. He cared for them and supported their families when they were sick or injured. More than could be said of the Government. Many a family was kept from the cold comfort of the 'Union' (workhouse) by the gang's free trading. One could almost say he performed a civic duty and should be hailed as a local benefactor! In the days before the welfare state that England has since become, Ransley and his like, were providing a valuable service and giving the common man a means of improving his lot. But the Government would not have seen it in quite that way!

On the 9th of September 1828, Elizabeth Ransley, Rhoda Higgins, Frances Gilham, Mary Giles, Catherine Bailey and Sarah

Pierce, plus their thirty two children (between them), set sail on *the Harmony* for Hobart, to join their husbands. Rhoda Higgins spent some time in the ships hospital with Dysenteria, a purging bowel infection.   George Ransley junior had a spell in there also with Opthalmia, an eye infection which seemed to be rife on board, as Sarah Pierce was also admitted with it. Later she also suffered Dysenteria. On the 10th of October, little Elizabeth Ransley, Bet's youngest child, was admitted to the ship's hospital under the care of ship's surgeon, Mr. William Clifford. This was as the ship was passing the Isle of St Jago. It was her old problem of swollen belly, purging, loss of appetite and debility. She was treated with warm baths, opium, arrow root and sage enemas with flannel rollers to the abdomen. This seemed to be the standard treatment of the time for any bowel disease. The little girl worsened and died on the 18th of October. She was nearly 22 months old. George probably never saw this youngest child! Having her family (sister and sister in law) and friends on board with her must have been some comfort to poor Bet at this very distressing time. They arrived in Hobart on the 14th of January 1829.

What happened next?

A brief account of those concerned in this drama

James Wilson

James was born in Mersham on 18th March 1798 to Elizabeth Wilson - there is no record of his father. He died on board the Leviathan on 15th February 1827 just days after arriving on board. He left his Mother behind, alone, in Aldington.

Richard Higgins

Richard was married to Rhoda Bailey, Bet's sister. His conduct on the hulk was good and very orderly on the ship. He was described as having left a wife and two children at Bilsington. Brought up in Bonnington he had a bastardy order taken out against him by Rhoda in October 1818 for support of a male child. This was Edward who died in January 1819 aged just 4 months. Richard and Rhoda lived apart but were clearly no strangers as she made another Bastardy order against him in May 1821, this time for a daughter, Jane, who survived. They married three years later in Bilsington, and had another daughter.

Rhoda travelled out in 1829 on the *Harmony.* She spent 10 days in the ships hospital with dysentery, where the ships surgeon described her as a 34 year old thin woman of relaxed habit who showed signs of having had many children! Interestingly she only had two by Richard at the time of his transportation. Richard was assigned to his wife in 1830 and granted a ticket of leave in 1833. He was arrested for sheep stealing in 1837, finally being pardoned on the 15th of May 1839. In the meantime their family grew with four more children being born.

It appears they were not very financially well off. Ten acres of their land had to be auctioned to settle defaulted mortgage payments after his death.

Richard died in August 1841 aged just 45, after being run over by a cart at Tea Tree. He sustained crush injuries to his chest from the cart wheels and his inquest describes "accidental death".

Rhoda married a John Poole a few years after Richard's death and died herself in 1862.

Thomas Gilham

Frances Gilham and her numerous children were the last to leave the vessel, having been detained until the 7th of February. They were kept on board due to Thomas Gilham's failure to arrive from the interior to collect them or to send a vehicle to convey them to his employer's place of residence. This would have been an interesting meeting as Frances had with her an eight month old daughter that she would have to explain to Thomas. Thomas had been apart from her for over seventeen months by that time! He would, in turn, have to explain his delay in collecting them.

Thomas was described as being five feet seven and a half inches tall with brown hair and hazel eyes. Aged 24, he had a scar on the outside of his left arm, a mole on the front of his neck and another on his shoulders. He left his wife and children at Aldington (spelt Allington on the handwritten reports - the Kentish dialect perhaps?)

Thomas went on to be assigned as servant to his wife and was described as a farmer. He received a ticket of leave in June 1833 and a conditional pardon in January 1839. Thomas and Frances must have reconciled as they went on to have seven more children. He could neither read nor write but went on to invest in property and ended up owning forty eight acres and a huge house with stables and numerous outbuildings - the wages of crime? He died from "natural decay" on the 5th of May 1865

Charles Giles

Charles was appointed to the field police just three months after his arrival in Hobart. He always explained the scar on his neck from being shot by the blockaders as "the effects of a blister." He was described as being very orderly on the ship across, and of good behaviour on the hulk, with a wife and children and a father and mother at Bilsington. Mary joined him in the January of 1829 and brought their three daughters with her. They went on to have a son, Charles Chapman Giles, and two more daughters, Mary and Harriet. Charles reverted to his old trade of shoemaker. Sadly Mary Giles senior died in June 1839. Charles remarried and went on to have several more children. He died in 1874 aged 76 following a long and painful illness.

Thomas Denard

Thomas was a cousin to the Bailey's. He owned land at Aldington Fright and kept two or three horses before his conviction. In the June of 1838 the 35 year old Thomas married 16 year old Ellen McCabe, a 'native of Tasmania'. They went on to have eight children, two of whom died in infancy. Ellen died in 1852 following the birth of her last daughter. She was aged just thirty. Aged 24 when he arrived in Van Diemen's Land, he is described as five feet seven inches with hazel eyes and brown hair. He had a scar in the centre of his forehead and one on the left side of his neck with a mole under the right side of his jaw. Thomas died in Victoria in 1880 aged 76 years. He was listed as an Immigrant and labourer.

James Smeed

James had been the instrument which had brought about the gang's demise. He had introduced firearms to them. Rumour had it that he had been a member of the North Kent gang before they were "smashed up" and some of their member's executed. He had then escaped over to the Marshes, bringing his old gang's ruthless methods and practices with him. He was one of the youngest members being only 22 when they were arrested. When giving evidence against the gang at their trial, Edward Horne had claimed that "only the big chaps had carried firearms and pretty big chaps they were too!"

He was described as five feet seven inches tall with brown hair and grey eyes. He had high cheek bones and a scar on the forefinger of his left hand. His hulk report was good and he was reported to have been very orderly on the prison ship, he was described as single. He too joined the field police, but in the July of 1830 he was fined for drunkenness and, in 1831, he was dismissed for gross disobedience of orders. In 1835 he was again working as a constable and was awarded sixty three pounds six shillings and eight pence with a free pardon for his role in apprehending two notorious bushrangers, Jeffkins and Brown. The report in the Hobart Town Courier of the 6th of February 1835 tells it all:

They accidentally met two miserable looking creatures, half emaciated, in most wretched attire. They had worn-out moccasins on their feet, and the one had an old blanket wrapped around him, with holes for his arms, while the other was clothed with an old grey jacket, put on as trousers, the sleeves serving to cover the thighs. They were however well armed, and immediately bid the constables defiance. They proved to be Brown and Jeffkins: Smith stepped forward calling on them to surrender, when he received a shot in the breast from Brown which killed him on the spot. Jeffkins also fired and wounded Buckley severely in the arm, who notwithstanding returned the fire and mortally wounded his antagonist, while Smeed levelled at Jeffkins and shot him dead. Brown was then secured, and is now lodged in Launceston hospital.

A week later, the *Courier*'s report from a member of the coronial jury provided further detail:

Jeffkins, after Brown fell, got behind a tree and fired at the constables, one of whom named Smeed took a circuit round and fired at Jeffkins, shooting him right through the head.

A little reparation for former crimes perhaps? He resigned from the police force in November 1836 and moved to Victoria. He appears to have become a cattle drover and died in 1882 in South Australia.

Paul Pierce

Paul was the son of the innkeeper at the Blue Anchor just outside Ruckinge. (This existed as a hostelry until 2017, now, sadly, no longer open for business.) Born in Canterbury around 1794, he was married to Sarah and they had seven children at the time of his arrest. He was listed as a gardener, but was also very skilled at grafting hops. He was described as being 34 years old, five feet four inches tall, with brown hair, grey eyes and scars and tattoos on his arms. The tattoos were 'hearts and darts, laurel and faint hearts' plus a huge scar on his right arm plus a mermaid and some faint marks on his left arm. He had owned a very old house and was reported to have hidden up his chimney and then climbed onto his roof in Bonnington during the first round of October arrests. He was taken on a wild stormy night in November along with Richard Higgins, John Bailey and Edward Pantry. As stated in the book, Pantry was to turn Kings Evidence dooming his friends to the noose at worst, transportation for life at best!

While Paul was halfway through his journey, his baby son Charles died. Three days after his arrival in Van Diemen's Land, his daughter, Delia, died. 1827 was a tragic year all round for the people of Aldington and surrounding villages! Sarah and their remaining four children joined him, with the other wives, in 1829. Travelling on the *Harmony,* they set sail a month before Paul had even applied for them to join him. On the 5th day of February 1828, Paul Pierce was reported for 'indecent and immoral conduct with Elizabeth Frankland in the service of his master'. Elizabeth's record confirms this offence. The records are difficult to read but it seems that, while Paul was reprimanded, Elizabeth was confined in a cell on bread and water for seven days. He was assigned to his wife on the 10th of July 1830. They went on to have two more children. He was granted a ticket of leave in 1833 and a conditional pardon in 1840.

Sarah died of consumption in 1848 and Paul died in October 1864 aged 80 years.

James Quested

Thirty five years old on his arrival in Van Diemen's Land, his report from both the hulk and the transport ship were "orderly". He was described as five feet seven and a quarter inches with grey eyes, brown hair and with a small scar on his left wrist. He obtained his conditional discharge in March 1837. James seems to have done rather well. He had two sons, one of whom became a schoolmaster. The other became Captain of a schooner. James died on the 29th of October 1877 due to age and infirmity. He was aged 85.

James Hogben

Aged 41 when arrested, he left a wife and seven children at Folkestone. His report on the hulk was 'good' and 'very orderly and correct' on the *Governor Ready*. He did have to wait an extra four years for his pardon and freedom as he had attempted an escape. In 1843 he was given his conditional discharge. Little is known of him after his pardon. He was described as a gardener and died on 22nd May 1858 aged 73.

Richard and William Wire

There is record of them both arriving in Hobart, then no further news. **Richard** was christened in Aldington on the 18th of August 1805. On Transportation he was aged 22 and is described as five feet seven and a half inches tall with grey eyes and brown hair. He had a small scar on his right wrist joint and one on his left ring finger as well as two moles on his left arm. **William,** aged 19, had been christened in Aldington on the 26th of June 1808. He had scars on his left little finger and wrist. He had hazel eyes, brown hair and was five feet seven inches tall. Since they were farm hands in Kent, it is probable that they were assigned to a farmer. Their conditional discharge came in May 1839. It has not been possible to discover if this is our Aldington lad, but a William Wires died in Brighton, Tasmania on the 30th of December 1845. His death is listed as erysipelas and his occupation was listed as a farmer. If this was our William, and it seems likely that it was, he would only have been 36. If that were true, poor Richard; as there is no record of either of them marrying. Brighton is about 23 kilometres from New Norfolk. It seems that Richard died from apoplexy in New Norfolk Tasmania in December 1888 aged 83. He was described as a pauper. It is hoped that poor Richard did not feel too lost without his younger brother.

John and Samuel Bailey

After their safe arrival in Hobart not much news could be found of them. **John** is described as having a large mole on his left arm, a scar on his thumb, left hand scar on the little finger, left hand scar on the forefinger, right hand scar on the middle finger, and two scars on his left cheek. He was estimated to be aged 34 years and was a whopping six feet one inch. He had a farm and kept several teams of horses, so he undoubtedly prospered. They gained their freedom with the usual Bailey luck and fortitude. **Samuel** is described as 41 years old, five feet eleven inches (the Bailey men were exceptionally tall for the times) with 2 scars on his left thumb. There was an incident in 1837 when they were accused of stealing some wheat from a farmer, but they seem to have been cleared. Samuel was given a conditional discharge in November 1839 and died in 1866 aged 79 - of "old age and infirmity". John, Uncle to Bet Ransley and Samuel Bailey was given a conditional discharge in May 1838.

George Ransley

George bore his miserable time on the hulk with his usual courage and spirit with which he faced everything - bravely and with strength. Fortunately their time on the hulk was short. Just eight weeks or so (some convicts spent months or even years in those terrible wretched conditions).

Once on board *the Governor Ready*, the men were treated far better and conditions were of a higher standard than some of the Navy sailors enjoyed.

Having lost a child he never grew to know, as well as his home and his dignity, it might be said that George had repaid any debt he owed to society. On the 30th January 1833, George was assigned to his wife, meaning they could live together. In 1838 he was granted a conditional pardon (meaning he could never return to England.) Being comparatively young and strong he would do well. He rented 500 acres and settled down to farm them, himself becoming master of convict servants.

He died aged 77, much loved and respected by many, to be followed by Elizabeth a few years later. His cause of death is recorded as "yellow jaundice", so it was likely to have been either pancreatic or liver cancer.

Their memorial in St John the Evangelist Church, Plenty, Tasmania, tells us that George was buried on the 29th of October 1856 and Elizabeth on the 1st January of 1859.

On his arrival he was described as being aged 45 years in 1827. He was five feet six and three quarter inches tall with brown hair, blue eyes and a double row of teeth in his top jaw. His behaviour on the *Governor Ready* was descried as very orderly and correct. He had a scar on his left thumb and forefinger. So many of the Blues had scars on their left hands. From the sharp knives used by right-handed men to cut the tubs free perhaps? In Lord Teignmouth's book, The Smugglers, George is described as a fine looking man, possessed of great muscular strength. He also tells us that he wore Gabardine mostly. This was the long smock worn almost sixty years or so before Thomas Burberry invented the waterproof Gaberdine fabric of the similar name, that we know today. Teignmouth also describes him as appearing in court in a fustian shooting jacket -his Sunday best perhaps? What I found particularly moving was his description in the Tasmanian records of his situation. It reads: "I had a family of my own. I left a wife and children in Bilsington parish. Samuel Bailey on board is my wife's brother. Married, 10 children, Protestant and a farmer/ploughman"

It is the past tense "had" that pulls at my heartstrings. He clearly didn't know if or when he would see them all again at that point. He was never to see his youngest child, Elizabeth, since she died at sea.

Certainly he was charismatic and must have had an attraction, as he seemed to have made friends from all stations of life. He inspired great loyalty from his smuggling colleagues. He seems to have been popular locally as well. There is absolutely nothing to hint that he was anything other than a faithful husband and a devoted father and good provider for his family. He appears to have been happy in

Tasmania with Elizabeth. It should be mentioned that she was four months pregnant with Matilda, their eldest daughter, when they married. This seems to have been the norm amongst the working classes in those days since a lot of George's associates married after Bastardy Charges had been brought against them! It would take either a reckless man or a fool, and George was neither, to get a Bailey woman pregnant and not marry her with the Bailey father and brothers to contend with!

Back home in Kent

Ralph Pepworth Hougham - Surgeon to the Blues

1827 was a miserable year all round for much of the Aldington area. When the Blues were deported some fifty children were left without a father and, in many cases, any income. The Parish had to step in to help and, for some, families were reliant on kindly relatives for support.

Ann Parkins, the wife of Ralph Hougham, surgeon to the Blues, had borne him 14 children. She died on the 17th of February 1827. She was five years older than he and had buried five of her children. She died exhausted at the age of just 47.

His mourning was brief for, by the November of that year, Ralph had married a Miss Charlotte Lee from Folkestone, who bore him another seven children, five of whom survived.

After the departure of the Blues, business dried up somewhat for Ralph. His ever growing family made huge financial demands on him and a small village practice did not pay the bills. Slowly he descended back to the penurious state he had been in when George had first employed him.

In April 1837, just 10 years after the Blues were transported, his house was stripped and all his goods sold at auction under an execution order to cover his debts. He came back to his house, went into his dispensary and took a phial of poison which he drank. He was buried in St Augustine's churchyard on the 3rd of April 1837, aged 51 years.

Lieutenant Samuel Hellard RN

He was the architect of George's downfall. After fulfilling his promise to avenge Richard Morgan's death by bringing the Blues to justice, he continued serving with the coastal blockade. He became Commander Hellard in 1830 following 30 years' service. He then transferred to the Coastguard and was posted to Ireland to supervise famine relief. There he died in 1840 of typhoid fever whilst on active service.

Edward Horne

Came from Ruckinge, and was reported to have been one of the worst of the gang. Shortly after turning King's Evidence, he was arrested for horse stealing and transported before the Blues even left the hulks! His £100 reward money did him no good at all.

John Horne

He was also from Ruckinge. He was arrested for sheep stealing and transported just a year after the Blues.

Edward Pantry

He was from Aldington. Within a year of the trial he was arrested for sheep stealing. He stole two sheep from a farm in Bonnington. He was seen by the brother of one of the transported Blues - it may have been a brother of Richard Higgins - who the following morning, a Sunday, reported him to the farmer. On the Monday morning about twenty locals were out after him (the Blues had been popular). Pantry was out harvesting when Constable Stokes came up and arrested him. Seeing the crowd were with the law this time, he offered no resistance. His house had been searched and they found the skin of a sheep. He was tried at Dymchurch and transported.

William Marsh

Took his £130 reward money and disappeared from the area – a wise move, you may say!

James Spratford

Having decided to brazen it out in the village, he invested his £130 reward money in one of the new horse drawn threshing machines. He worked this until 1830, when, as he had made himself even more unpopular, he was one of the first victims of the Swing riots. Targeting him deliberately, the local farm labourers rioted for higher wages and completely destroyed his machine along with singing and the shouting of jovial remarks! (Much good did his treachery do him!) Some of the local rioters came up in front of Sir Edward Knatchbull, the local magistrate, for their part in this. He sentenced them to a very lenient three days in prison. Both he and the jury were rebuked afterwards for allowing such a soft sentence!

Sir Edward Knatchbull 9th Baronet P.C. F.R.S.

Knatchbull was the son of Sir Edward Knatchbull, 8th Baronet, and Mary, daughter of William Western Hugessen. He was educated at Christ Church, Oxford and matriculated in 1800. He was called to the Bar at Lincoln's Inn in 1803. In 1819 he succeeded in the baronetcy on the death of his father.

Edward was elected as Member of Parliament (MP) for Kent in November 1819, to fill the vacancy caused by the death of his father. He held the seat until the 1831 general election, which he did not contest. The Reform Act 1832 split the Kent county constituency into Eastern and Western divisions and, at the 1831 general election, he was elected as one of the two MPs for the new Eastern division of Kent.

He served under Sir Robert Peel as Paymaster of the Forces between 1834 and 1835 and as Paymaster-General between 1841 and 1845.

Edward married twice. His first wife was Annabella Christiana Honywood, the daughter of Sir John Honywood, 4th Baronet. They married on the 25th of August 1806, and had six children. Annabella died in childbirth in 1814 and on the 24th of October 1820, Edward married Fanny Catherine Knight, daughter of Edward Knight (née Edward Austen, the brother of English novelist Jane Austen). They had nine children. He died in May 1849, aged 67, at the family's Mersham Hatch estate in Kent. He was succeeded in the baronetcy by his son from his first marriage, Norton. Lady Knatchbull died in December 1882.

The Hatch at Mersham is still owned by Knatchbull family. Latterly it was home to Lady Patricia Knatchbull, 2nd Countess

Mountbatten of Burma, third cousin to Queen Elizabeth II, who died on the 13th of June 2017.

John Knatchbull

(c. 1791 – 13 February 1844)

He was the brother to Edward. At one time he was a naval captain and finally a convict who was found guilty of murder in 1844. He was one of the earliest to raise in a British court the plea of moral insanity (unsuccessfully).

He was born in Mersham, Kent, The son of Sir Edward Knatchbull 8th Baronet of Mersham Hatch. He attended Winchester College and volunteered for the navy in 1804, serving until 1818 and rising to the rank of a captain. In December 1813 he was commissioned to command *Doterell*, but missed the ship and was reappointed in September 1814. After the Battle of Waterloo in June 1815, the navy was reduced and he was retired on full pay until March 1818, when his pay was stopped by the Admiralty because of a debt he had incurred in the Azores.

In August 1824 he was found guilty of stealing with force and arms at the Surrey Assizes under the name of John Fitch. Knatchbull was given a 14-year sentence and transported to New South Wales on the *Asia*.

On 31st of December 1831 he was charged with forging Judge Dowling's signature to a cheque on the Bank of Australia - the forged note was an exhibit for the prosecution. He was found guilty in the February of 1832 and sentenced to death. This sentence was commuted to transportation for seven years to Norfolk Island.

Whilst on Norfolk Island, he took part in two mutinies. On the way to Norfolk Island in 1832 Knatchbull conspired with other convicts on board ship to poison the crews' and guards' food with arsenic. The mutineers were informed on and the arsenic was found, but it was seen as too much trouble to return the prisoners to the mainland for trial and they became known among their fellow convicts as "Tea-Sweeteners". In the second mutiny of 1834 planned against the governor of the convict settlement and his deputy, Knatchbull escaped punishment by informing on his fellow mutineers.

In January 1844 he murdered shopkeeper Ellen Jamieson with a tomahawk while stealing money for his upcoming marriage. He was tried on 24 January and found guilty of murder and sentenced to be hanged.

During the early part of 1844, in Sydney, a Norfolk Island expiree, who held a ticket of leave, had gone into the shop of a poor widow, named Ellen Jamieson, and asked for some trifling article. As Mrs. Jamieson served him, he raised a tomahawk in his hand, and clove the unfortunate woman's head in a savage manner. She lingered for a few days, and died, leaving two orphaned children.

An attempt was made to set up a plea of insanity for John; a barrister being employed by the agent for the suppression of capital punishment. But, and I quote, *so foul a villain could not be saved from the gallows.* It is gratifying to add that Sir Edward Knatchbull, the brother of the criminal, had sent out a handsome donation for the orphans of Mrs. Jamieson. Sir Edward also paid for their education.

John was sentenced to hang for the murder. The execution was to be held outside the gates of Darlinghurst gaol and was scheduled for 9a.m. At the crack of dawn scores of people, children included, were swarming across the racecourse towards Darlinghurst Hill. The *Australian* newspaper judged the throng to be 10,000 strong. Captain John Knatchbull, aged 56 years, was led out into Forbes Street, at the gaol gates on the Darlinghurst Ridge. Wearing genteel black broadcloth, Captain Knatchbull then "*ascended the fatal scaffold without trepidation or fear, and was launched into another world with a noble and fervent prayer trembling on his lips*". The bell of St Phillip's tolled thrice and John Knatchbull was dead.

John Ransley

In reality, John Ransley, youngest brother to the Rascally Brothers, was a quiet, well-disposed man, who led an exemplary life. I only "borrowed" him for my story! He married Elizabeth Velvitch in August 1818 and they had eight children, one of whom, Edward, died in 1843 aged just 5 years. A son, John, died in 1844 aged 20 years. They lived at Brabourne and are buried at Mersham - Elizabeth on September the 19th 1843 aged 46 years and John on January the 24th 1852 aged 59 years.

Juliet Knatchbull

Well, Juliet can become anything the reader wishes. She and her household are the only characters in this story who are wholly fictitious. She had, however, a very important role to play. She was the chain that linked it all together, the means of showing the complex and admirable personality of George. She could also bear testament to the complexity of the times they lived in. It was necessary to invent Juliet to explain the inexplicable – for example what was the relationship between Edward Knatchbull and George Ransley? What secrets did George know? How involved was Edward with the gang's nefarious activities (if at all)? We do not know this and cannot find it out, therefore Juliet's creation was needed in order for me to tell the story in a way that can offer a possible explanation and also as a way to capture the times a little more fully.

One does not normally think of a smuggler as the lover of a lady but, from what we glean from his personality, George could transcend any class or age division. Juliet seemed a good way to demonstrate that, whilst maintaining the traditional "love twist" to the tale! I am sure that if Juliet really had existed, she would have fallen hook, line and sinker for George's charms!

The last word

We will never see the like of the Aldington Blues again! Some say Cephas Quested had been their leader before George. Having read his description by Lord Teignmouth, I personally doubt it. He was an illiterate drunkard! However, it would suit the gang to let the authorities think that they had captured their leader. It was an ideal way to take the heat off them to some extent. I personally think, more realistically, that, initially, Bailey senior and, subsequently, George, would have been more suited to lead the gang.

It is interesting to note that most of the men had scars on their left hands, fingers or wrists. This must have been from working rapidly with sharp knives to cut the tubs free when unloading a cargo. It was reported that they worked with such speed that it was miraculous that no one lost a finger!

Most were described as "Protestant" and their descriptions of their birth places are rather quaint by the standards of today since they show the old Kentish dialect (having been written down phonetically by the records officers). George was born in "Rocking" which was his pronunciation of Ruckinge. The Wire brothers were born in "Allington" which is Kentish for Aldington. These details bring the Blues to life for me more than anything else.

Their exploits have to be taken in the context of the time. While some people may think the country better off without them and their crimes, they did bring prosperity to the area and to many a poor family. The average wage for an agricultural worker was about 12 to 13 shillings a week. Families were large and, if you were sick or injured, you had to rely on the kindness of your employer (or the parish workhouse) to get by.

Men returning from the Napoleonic wars were bored with the hard grind they returned to. Many of them wanted better and found it hard to settle into the dull routine and poverty of their previous lives. George paid his tub men eight shillings per run and twenty shillings per run to his batsmen plus the hard core of twenty or so gang members.

In an era where you could be hung for stealing a few paltry items or poaching a neighbour's sheep, the gang needed to protect themselves from capture. The carrying of the oak cudgels, or bats, was a precaution and they would only be used if necessary. George himself was never known to carry a gun and he drank hardly at all. Contemporary reports, however, do say that he could be as ruthless as the situation demanded. He inspired great loyalty in his men as he improved their lot immensely and employed lawyers to represent them if caught and tried. He employed a surgeon to care for them and supported their families financially if they were unable to work, or were imprisoned. This maintained the loyalty of all his men and their families. In a way, he was a local benefactor and, in the context of the times, should maybe have been given some civic award rather than exiled for life.

Some of the punishments meted out to convicts and criminals of all ages were draconian, and far worse than anything carried out by the Blues and their like.

Why did Sir Edward Knatchbull fight for the lives of the Blues? That is a question I would love to know the definitive answer to. Could George have known something against him or his family? Almost certainly Sir Edward was receiving uncustomed goods from the gang. He may even have been storing some of their contraband about his estates – indeed, there were numerous outbuildings. His career was blossoming; adverse publicity could do nothing but harm for the Knatchbulls at that time. John Knatchbull had caused them enough problems. If the Blues had faced execution they would have had nothing to lose by broadcasting any adverse intelligence about the family. Transportation of the gang would keep safe the reputation of the Knatchbulls in those days of slow news and travel. Being transported to the other side of the world was sufficient to render a man virtually dead to his erstwhile home in England - especially at a time when it took a minimum of three months to travel there by sail.

There is no doubt that George was a great leader of men. He had succeeded in everything he did. He was said to be a great horseman then a successful and popular 'free trader'. He became a popular employer and farmer in Van Diemen's Land. If he had been born into a different class, perhaps been given a better education and a different chance in life, who knows, he may even have been lauded and remembered with the likes of Nelson, or Wellington. They were, without doubt, the great Englishmen of their time. Instead George was banished from the land of his birth.

No, we will never see the likes of the 'Blues' again, but we can remember them. When visiting the Aldington area and the mediaeval churches on the Romney and Walland Marshes, it is still possible to feel their spirit emanating from the very earth. We may not see their like again, for certain, but we can at least rejoice that they once existed.

"Fear not for the future, weep not for the past"

Percy Bysshe Shelly

Since writing this I have, amazingly enough, made contact with some direct descendants of George Ransley living in Australia. They are lovely people and have been most helpful to me. They have given me facts, as they know them, about the family. I now have some useful links and information on George; in particular on his life in New Norfolk, Tasmania. I would like to thank Mark, Bruce and Sylvana Ransley for their help and for being patient enough to humour a complete stranger from England contacting them out of the blue on social media! I hope, one day soon, to visit Tasmania and to meet them all. It is a wondrous thing, almost two hundred years later, to be able to talk with direct descendants of that fascinating man and I certainly value their acquaintance

Bibliography

Archives Office of Tasmania

Tasmanian Archives online – Linc

The Wicked Trade – John Douch

The Smugglers (vol. 11) Lord Teignmouth and Charles G. Harper

From Quarterdeck to Gallows- John Knatchbull Narrative and retrospect Colin Roderick

Lynne's Family – Lynne's Tasmanian family online

Founders and Survivors (on line)

Ralph Rashleigh – James Tucker

The Ashford Museum (Kent)

Surgeons Journal from HMS Harmony 1827- Mr. William Clifford, ships surgeon

UK Prison Hulk registers and letter books – 1802 – 1849

Traders of the Fifth Continent (tales of Smugglers and Rascals on the Romney Marsh) – Lyn Watts

Kent online parish clerks – Executions at Maidstone 1735 – 1930 (for the Rascally Brothers)

Convict records of Australia

Old Bailey Proceedings – 1740 – 1913 (Cephas Quested)

About the Author

Lyn Watts worked in the National Health Service for 40 years. During this time she became experienced in most branches of nursing, eventually specialising in resuscitation and Life Support training. When she retired in 2014, she and I (also an NHS retiree) set up our own company, providing the same high-standard training to doctors, dentists and other healthcare professionals.

Lyn's work keeps her very busy, and most of her spare time is spent with her family, including her seven young grandchildren, and with her beloved horses and dogs. However, she somehow still finds time to write, mainly because she is not a huge fan of television.

This is the third book from Lyn. It is, however, her first long book – the other two being short stories, for which she is best known.

Lyn's research work is as important to her as the writings themselves and she tries to get the facts as accurate as possible in everything. She is widely read and the library at home has now extended into the loft. At the last count there were eleven bookcases in the house. The internet also provides valuable data and is an invaluable tool for any author these days. Lyn also has a wide experience of life. She has lived in Kent, London, Sussex and Somerset and has encountered people from all walks of life and they always give her pleasure (some when they enter the room, others when they leave!)

Stories continue to be written, so there will undoubtedly be further volumes to look forward to in the future. She is still being published regularly in magazines and enjoys the challenge of writing to a word count (usually very small) and then expanding those same stories for a wider, and less restricted, readership. I have had enormous pleasure in proof reading and editing this volume.

Charlie Watts. East Sussex January 2018

Also available by the same author

Traders of the Fifth Continent – Tales of Smugglers and Rascals on the Romney Marsh (March 2015) available at £5

The Dark Lantern (and other Tales)   19 short stories on a variety of subjects. (July 2016) available at £6

These are available from WattKnott Publishing

Testers, Whatlington, Battle, East Sussex TN33 0NS

Or email: lyncharliewatts@hotmail.co.uk

Prices include postage and packing

Both are also available from Ebay or Amazon

And all books are available on Kindle